SUDBURY

history & guide

SUDBURY

history & guide

Barry Wall

TEMPUS

frontispiece The magnificent Renaissance ceiling in St Gregory's church.

First published 2004

Tempus Publishing Ltd
The Mill, Brimscombe Port
Stroud, Gloucestershire GL5 2QG
www.tempus-publishing.com

British Library Cataloguing in Publication Data.
A catalogue record for this book is available from the British Library.

ISBN 0 7524 3317 2

Typesetting and origination by Tempus Publishing.
Printed in Great Britain

Contents

Acknowledgements

I would like to acknowledge assistance from the always helpful staff at the County Record Offices at Chelmsford, St Edmundsbury and Norwich. This book also contains some revised material from my own publication *Sudbury Through the Ages* (1984) published by East Anglian Magazine Ltd, Ipswich.

Colour section picture credits: all images by Sue Lui except 1, 10, 13, 17, 22 and 29 by Mick Lillie and 9, 11, 23, 25 and 26 by Sudbury History Society.

Black and white picture credits: images on pages 45, 53 (bottom), 54 (bottom) 60, 61, 66, 122 (top), 123, 124 by Sue Lui. Images on pages 42 and 43 by Mike Lillie.

Images on page 54 reproduced by permission of RCHME Crown Copyright. Those on pages 17 and 36 reproduced by kind permission of Simmons Aerofilms Ltd.

Introduction

It is over a century since the first history of Sudbury was written by F.C.D. Sperling based on the notes of W.W. Hodson and it has been out of print for most of that time. A second history of Sudbury was written jointly by Grimwood and Kaye in the 1950s and has never been reprinted. Both were notable works of their time and have been valuable sources for historians ever since, but the time is long overdue for a thoroughly researched and comprehensive up-to-date history of this most interesting of English towns. Meanwhile, to keep the kettle boiling, here is the story of Sudbury drawn from various sources and with additional material based on conclusions reached by myself after looking at the evidence to hand.

In 1983 I wrote *Sudbury Through the Ages*, in which the story of the town was told through its buildings and streets. A single paragraph concerning the De Clare family, drawn from nineteenth-century sources, is no longer accurate. The facts as given here reveal a much more interesting insight into the early medieval history of what was in fact a royal burgh. Sudbury was an isolated outpost of the Gloucester royal estate and although it passed by marriage to the De Clares the Crown never lost sight of it and in due course reclaimed it.

The significance of the Saxon Great Ditch created by the diversion of the river and the importance of Sudbury as a strategic defensive position against the Danes suggests another royal connection with Edward the Elder for the first time. Likewise the affect on Sudbury when Elizabeth De Burgh finally got control of her fortune in 1327 has never been considered before even though some of the town's finest features came about as a direct consequence.

St Peter's church has been re-evaluated and given more accurate dating which will explain certain inconsistencies which have troubled us before. Likewise we are now able to understand the significance of St Gregory's chancel now that we know it represents the chapel of the college and we can put a name to the builder. Furthermore, if Mr Peter Minter is correct with regard to the reused bricks in the tower, we have to reconsider the early history of brick making in this country yet again.

Sudbury is an extraordinary town with a long history which has emerged from the last century remarkably preserved in spite of a very shaky period in the 1960s and '70s. It is a Saxon and early medieval town whose street pattern evolved from those early years. Those streets were never intended for the traffic they have to contend with today. It is a great irony that had the bridge not been built the traffic would be obliged to take very nearly the route of the proposed and rejected bypass.

Nevertheless the photographs will show what a very pleasant town it is to live in and to visit. Those who know the town well will be aware that there have been some omissions but I hope nothing too serious. The book is about the town, what may not be apparent is the surrounding countryside, believe me it is beautiful too.

chapter one

Arrivals and departures

Around 2,000 BC a group of Early Bronze Age farmers settled on a hill above a loop in the River Stour, on the Suffolk side looking into what is now Essex. They cleared sufficient land to create small fields for growing crops. They had sheep and cattle that grazed on the low ground by the water's edge. The river then was broader and faster flowing and the sloping ground above the valley was covered in forest. They had chosen their site well, South facing and safely above the flood plain with ample fresh water springs and abundant supplies of timber. For countless generations these people enjoyed a modest but peaceful life. Fragments of their broken pottery and other artefacts which they cast into waste pits would re-emerge in AD 1977 to confirm their habitation and stake their claim as the first settlers on the hill which was to become Sudbury.

Later the hill became home for an Iron Age tribe who found it necessary to build a sequence of banks and ditches for their protection. They formed three sides of a rectangular encampment facing across the river towards Essex, from whence they were obviously expecting trouble. Who were these people? Suffolk and Norfolk was the territory of the Iceni, a tribe familiar to us through the exploits of their warrior Queen Boudicca. However, the Trinovantes whose capital was at Camulodunum fourteen miles away in Essex, had infiltrated into South Suffolk and it is more than likely that they were responsible for the earthworks.

Assuming that to be the case then the trouble they were expecting was from the invading Germanic tribe called the Belgae who were sweeping up from the South early in the first century BC. There is a large hill fort at Clare that was probably built for the same reason, and yet another, large Iron Age encampment has been identified a mile to the NE of Sudbury at Chilton and is awaiting further study. The next decade should provide us with a great deal more information to explain exactly what was happening in this vicinity at that crucial time in British history.

Seventeen years after the Roman invasion of AD 43 under Claudius, and after appalling treatment from the Romans, Boudicca led her people in a massive

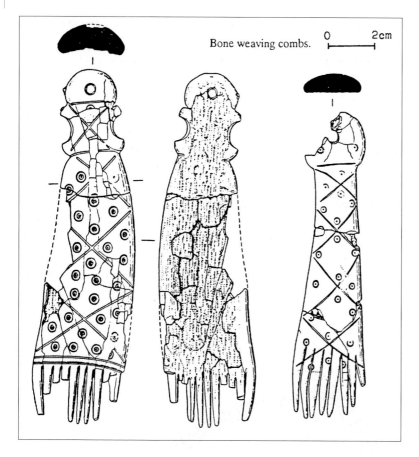

Bone weaving combs.   0   2cm

Iron Age bone weaving
combs found on the Stour
House site.

uprising against them. Other tribes joined her, including the Trinovantes from Essex, which would have included the group from Sudbury. They sacked Colchester, defeating the Ninth Legion, then went on to sack Verulamium (St Albans) and London. They came very close to ending Roman domination of Britain but were finally defeated in the Midlands.

These brave people left a permanent reminder of their presence in Sudbury. The banks with which they fortified their settlement exist as sharp inclines in the street pattern of the modern town. They can be seen in School Street, Plough Lane, Walnuttree Lane, The Croft and most dramatically in Stour Street.

A modest excavation in 1990 at the junction of Gregory Street and Stour Street, behind Stour House, recovered some highly decorated bone weaving combs, a bronze Late Iron Age 'button and loop' fastener for clothing, and most interestingly a collection of baked clay sling pellets. Two Iron Age ditches, each 3-4ft deep proved to be boundary ditches and not part of the defences. A parallel ditch close by was of later Romano-British origin but it was marked by a wooden post fence from the early medieval period and a flint and rubble wall from the fifteenth century. This is an extraordinary example of a property boundary being sustained for nearly 1,500 years.

Further trials on the South side of Walnuttree Lane, opposite the hospital, revealed very little because the site had been disturbed and plundered for gravel in the nineteenth century when Macadam was altering the gradient of Mill Hill. A large area of the encampment lies relatively undisturbed in the grounds of Walnuttree Hospital and awaits investigation in the not too distant future, when a new replacement hospital is built.

The Romano-British ditch mentioned above, together with a considerable quantity of re-used Roman brick and tile in the walls of St Gregory's and All Saints' churches, points conclusively to a continued habitation of the site. Even so, there is a disappointing paucity of finds from this period so far within the town. There is a stretch of Roman road outside the town and to the North of Chilton and archaeological field walks in the vicinity have proven that there was some considerable activity above the valley at that point. It is possible that there was a Romano-British settlement on the higher ground which became difficult to defend. There was certainly a large one at Long Melford, most of which lies buried beneath the medieval town on the West side of Hall Street.

What we are looking for is some clue to tell us when the Anglo Saxons moved on to the fortified hill and gave it a name, 'Sudburic' – 'Sudburgh' – Sudbury. The name describes the place aptly: Sud (South) burgh (fortified town). There has been much debate concerning the prefix Sud or South. In relation to

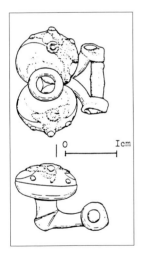

above Late Iron Age bronze fastener, probably for a cloak, from the Stour House site.

right Plan of Sudbury showing the Saxon Ditch and Rampart.

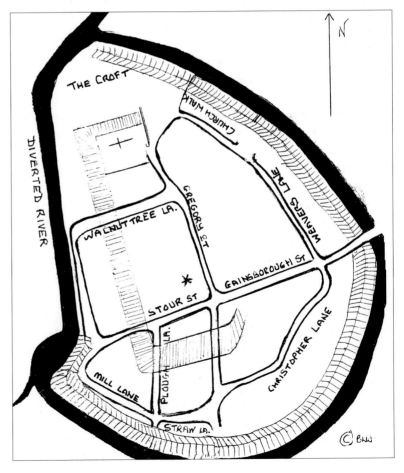

where? Norwich, St Edmundsbury and Thetford have been suggested. It probably simply identifies the geographic position of the town within the kingdom of East Anglia and Suffolk. Had it been built on Ballingdon Hill in Essex the East Saxons would have named it Northburgh.

Saxons had attacked these shores during the Roman occupation as early as the third century, hence the shore forts at Walton and Felixstowe which were intended to defend the river estuaries. In the late fourth century, pagan Saxons from North Germany were eventually settled in parts of East Anglia, but nothing has yet been found to connect them with Sudbury at such an early date.

During the eighth century the old kingdom of East Anglia formed part of Mercia and it was then, in 797-98, when Sudbury is mentioned in the *Anglo Saxon Chronicle*. The item is brief and informs us that Bishop Aelfhun of East Anglia died here. This is the first documentary evidence or naming of a Saxon township in Suffolk. More than that it is an indication of a Christian settlement worthy of a visit of such importance. We know that St Gregory's church was a Saxon foundation and was well established by 970 and 993 when it is mentioned in wills.

The church was built within the defences on a site close to the Northern embankment. Like the homes of the people it was probably a simple timber construction at first. However, at a later date the Saxons rebuilt their church in flint and brick which was a sign of prosperity and stability. This brings us to The Great Ditch, described as such in a document dated 1318 in the archives at Westminster Abbey relating to St Bartholomew's Priory, and cited as a property boundary within the later medieval town.

The Great Ditch and Rampart was an impressive earthwork built by the Saxons to completely encircle the town that had expanded way beyond the old Iron Age defences. It was to mark the confines of the town until the fourteenth century and today's street pattern within the old town is a direct consequence of it. The date of its construction was unknown and an attempt to determine it was taken in 1992-93 at a section in Mill Lane.

The excavation was carried out under the direction of Stuart Boulter of the Fields Project Division of the Archeological Unit associated with the Suffolk County Planning Department. The opportunity arose following the demolition of the nineteenth-century school buildings prior to the construction of a new school. It was the first time ever that a site had become available for examination on the line of the ditch to determine its size and age and when it was filled in. Unfortunately its age was not determined.

The profile and dimensions of the ditch, at least this section of it, were revealed and were surprising. It was 21 metres wide and 3 metres deep with a flat bottom and sloping sides. It was estimated that the upcast, or soil removed from the ditch, would have formed a rampart on the town side 15 metres wide at the base, 6 metres in height with an angled slope of 40 degrees. This would have created a most effective defensive barrier. It would seem that there was one main entrance through the rampart into the town where present day Gainsborough Street begins, at the foot of Market Hill.

opposite Plan of Sudbury from around 1200 showing the expansion of the parish of All Saints beyond the ditch. Modern street names are used. This street plan, the historic core of modern Sudbury, has remained intact ever since with the exception of Mill Lane which has been replaced with a diverted footpath. One can plainly see why Christopher Lane was called Wylewerlelane, every other street or lane either follows the curve of the ditch or is straight, indicating a planned Saxon town, almost certainly by Edward the Elder in around 911-17.

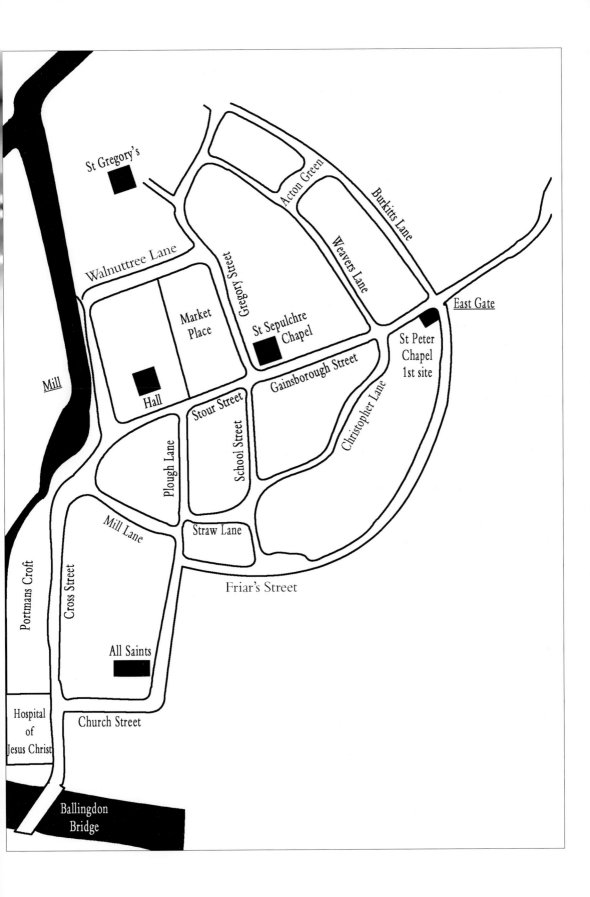

One can walk the course of the ditch today from The Croft then following Croft Road, Burkitt's Lane, Friar's Street, through the school in Church Street, it then enters the river at Garden Place in Cross Street. A large section survives in the form of the Mill Leet that runs along the foot of The Croft towards North Meadows. This section of the river is entirely man made. The old course of the river flows behind Fulling Pit meadow opposite The Croft.

Within the ramparts there were two main thoroughfares, East to West with Gainsborough Street and Stour Street, North to South with Gregory and School Streets. Christopher Lane, Weaver's Lane and Straw Lane backed on to the Rampart.

The digging of the ditch, which included the diversion of the river, was a massive task requiring considerable resources of manpower and funds. It raises questions as to why such a strong fortification was deemed necessary at this particular place and who could have ordered its construction. The fact that a mint was established here during the time of Aethelred II, (The Unready) 966-1016, who spent his entire reign fighting off marauding Danes, suggests that they may have been the attackers. Certainly Kent, Essex and Suffolk were the targets in 99l. The same year in which a decision was made to raise £10,000 in taxes to pay the Danes to go home, it was called Danegeld. The tax was on land with tough penalties for defaulters.

The Danes naturally returned to maraud again and again. In 1004 they sacked Norwich and Thetford to the North of the county but there is no record of them entering Sudbury. At Little Cornard however there is more than a hint of a skirmish with Dane's Hole, Killingdown Hill, and Sharpfight Meadow all adjacent and backed up with the discovery of a Danish sword and shield in the nineteenth century. In 1013 they were back again, this time to conquer.

Aethelred did indeed build a few Burghs which were intended as military forts for local strategic defence but I do not think Sudbury was one of them. It makes more sense to attribute the work to Edward the Elder (872-924), the eldest son of Alfred the Great. He was King of Wessex and, jointly with his sister, Ethelflaed 'Lady of the Mercians', engaged in a successful series of campaigns against the Danes throughout 909-20. To this purpose he built or strengthened nearly thirty Burghs but these were not merely for military use. Many of them were also for civilian occupation as towns with street plans.

In 911 he built the Burgh at Hertford and the following year was moving against the Danes in Essex and creating Burghs at Witham and Maldon (916) and strengthening the defences at Colchester. By 917 he was in control of East Anglia and the West Saxons had completely taken over Mercia. Of all the Saxon kings he is by far the most likely candidate to have had the resources and the impetus to strengthen and fortify Sudbury at some time between 911 and 917.

At the time of the Norman Conquest the town was owned by the mother of the powerful Earl Morcar. It was forfeited to King William I and it stayed with the Crown until Henry I gave it to his own illegitimate son Robert, Earl of Gloucester. It is not clear when the gift was made but presumably it was after the drowning of Henry's only legitimate son in the *White Ship* disaster of 1120.

chapter two

Gloucester to Clare, 1120-1314

Robert of Gloucester had all the attributes required for kingship except legitimacy. After his father died he was immensely wealthy with most of his lands in the West Country. During the next reign his loyalty was severely divided between Stephen and Matilda as the country went through turmoil after seventy years of strong Norman government.

The Earl of Gloucester's fortified town with its flourishing market was prospering rather well. The coins minted in the town bear the name SUDBY on the reverse which is a strong indication that a fair amount of trade and industry was going on outside the town. Towards the North, was a large expanse of woodland which was a valuable asset to the Earl and would be the source of timber for the further expansion of Sudbury in later years. In this vicinity a new manor would soon be formed from whence future Stewards would keep an eye on the town and it would be called Woodhall.

In the years 1114-16, Wulfric the Moneyer, the man in charge of the Mint, was ready to retire having made quite a lot of money in all senses of the phrase. He founded a small Benedictine cell or priory that he presented to Westminster Abbey, a place he would have been familiar with on his trips to London connected with his work. The priory was dedicated to St Bartholomew and built on land close to the Earl's Wood. Subsequent events were to prove that it was built of timber although more substantial buildings would be erected at a later date. Wulfric retired to Westminster where he became a monk and one assumes he was eventually buried there.

When the earl died in 1147 the town passed to his son, William FitzRobert, Earl of Gloucester, who also took his responsibilities with regard to Sudbury very seriously. Although still confined within its ditch and ramparts there was pressure to expand. The church was too small to cope with its enlarged congregation but rather than destroy an obviously revered building, William founded a new 'chapel of ease' near the town gate, within the Rampart, and dedicated to St Peter. He then presented the advowson of both church and chapel to the Nunnery at Eaton in Warwickshire

Perhaps the most significant inconvenience was the approach to the town from London and Essex. Ballingdon was little more than a hamlet centred around a green on the road from Henny and Middleton to Borley. Between the hamlet and Sudbury, apart from the river, was an area of marshland. Ballingdon Hill as a thoroughfare did not exist. To reach Sudbury from Essex the early traveller made his way from Bulmer Tye to Bulmer Street thence via Smeetham Hall Lane to what is now a footpath beside Brundon Wood.

The nucleus of the Saxon and Norman village of Brundon was with its church beside the wood. The last remnants were seen in the mid-nineteenth century. From here they would descend into the valley to cross the river at Brundon Mill where there was a ford within yards of the King's highway (Melford Road) that would lead them into Sudbury through the East Gate. By a curious coincidence they would have followed very nearly the route of the proposed new by-pass.

The expansion of the town beyond the ditch and the much-needed bridge across the Stour were delayed until after Stephen's death in 1154. When stability returned under Henry II work on both projects commenced.

A section of the rampart to the south of the town was removed and the ditch at that point filled in. This allowed the creation of a new parish formed by Cross Street and Church Street. It forms a loop, much like the outer bailey of a great castle. For this new parish beyond the town a church was built dedicated to All Saints, before 1183, when it was sold to St Alban's Abbey.

No expense was spared with regard to the bridge and the construction of the causeway across the marshes. The stone was brought across the channel from Caen in Normandy, which is not surprising since the quarry was owned by the family. In any case it would have been just as costly to bring suitable stone across land from the Midlands or the West Country. The bridge had eight arches resting on boat-shaped cutwaters and was to last for nearly 500 years. The causeway with its system of drainage ditches from the bridge to the hamlet at the foot of the hill became Ballingdon Street eventually. A thoroughfare was then opened from the hamlet direct to Bulmer Tye. This would have been done with the co-operation of the neighbouring landowners, chiefly the Earl of Oxford, fortunately a friend of the Gloucesters.

Most of the ditch was probably filled in by the end of the century but a document relating to a property transaction, dated 24 July 1318, makes it clear that part was still exposed: '...at the great ditch between land formerly of William Turk and of Adam Pake, abutting one end on the ditch, the other on land formerly of Robert of Barton'. Unfortunately the site cannot be identified. One section, created by the diversion of the river, was adapted to form a mill leet that still exists today.

The Chapel of the Holy Sepulchre

In 1173 William founded and built a chapel by the market place at the centre of the town that he dedicated to the Holy Sepulchre. He endowed it with land

The southern loop of Cross Street and Church Street formed when the bridge was built. This created the new Parish of All Saints. Behind Cross Street is the Common known as Portmanscroft, part of the Freemen's Little and Great Common.

outside the town but it served no parish and appears to have remained a private chapel until the Reformation.

The dedication suggests that it was founded by William in lieu of a trip to the Holy Land. Over the years there has been some confusion with this chapel and the hospital founded by his daughter Amicia. They were two foundations on different sites though nothing survives of either. However an observant builder with an interest in local history gave the following account to a meeting of the Suffolk Archaeological Institute in 1853:

The exact site of the chapel of Holy Sepulchre I had the good fortune to ascertain in 1826, when employed by the late Samuel French to build three houses at the upper end of, and fronting Sepulchre Street to the south, the west end abutting upon Gregory Street.

Upon excavating the soil for the cellarage at about seven feet below the surface of the footpath, I found eight human skeletons each lying due east and west and a few feet distant from each other. Continuing the excavation to the north side for the back foundation, I found, about eighteen inches below the surface, a part of one of the northern buttresses, in height about four feet, and nearly three feet in thickness, composed of quarry stones at the angles and the other parts of pit stones strongly cemented with liquid grout, i.e. lime and gravel. It was broken in pieces and used in the foundations.

The distance from the street to the buttress was about 23ft to its northern or outer side, so that the skeletons must have been interred in the interior of the chapel, which supposing it to have been 40 or 50ft in breadth, must have covered the space where the highway is now.

The chapel was probably only half the width suggested, which would make it about the size of St Bartholomew's, approximately 20ft. Otherwise it is an excellent report of a very interesting discovery. Sepulchre Street was renamed Gainsborough Street in the early twentieth century. Sadly we have no idea whose bones they were or what became of them. We do know that the chapel was presented to the Priory at Stoke-by-Clare just as the advowson of St Gregory's was given to the Nunnery at Eaton earlier.

Shortly before his death in 1183 William presented Sudbury to his daughter Amicia as part of her marriage settlement when she became the wife of Richard de Clare, 3rd Earl of Hertford, whose castle was about twelve miles upstream at Clare. Sudbury was to become part of the great Honour of Clare – but not just yet.

Amicia's marriage to Richard of Clare produced one son, Gilbert, then difficulties arose. By 1198 they were separated on the grounds of consanguinity. Amicia retained her Gloucester estates and titles that her son would inherit on her death. Richard died in 1217 which was also the year in which she founded her hospital at the foot of Ballingdon Bridge.

The hospital, dedicated to Jesus Christ and the Blessed Virgin Mary, was most generously endowed with the tithe of her mills in Sudbury, five acres of arable land, one acre of meadow and one of pasture in the King's Marsh, the right of pasturage for four cows and twenty sheep in Kings Marsh and Portmans Croft, the Bridge Tolls, and the rents of fifteen houses in the new quarter. She stipulated that neither she nor her heirs would put any person into the hospital without permission of the people of Sudbury.

The stipulation seems to confirm that the town had achieved some form of self government with the consent of its aristocratic overlords. There is some evidence from documents at this time that many of the leading townspeople were also members of Amicia's entourage. This close intimacy with their lady may well have arisen because of her estrangement from her husband and presumably the fact that she was resident in Sudbury and not Clare. However, the same close relationship would emerge again under another Lady, Elizabeth De Burgh, in the next century.

Another sign of the growing independence of the town is the fact that, although Sudbury formed part of the Hundred of Thingoe, (the other part

Floodgate Walk, Sudbury.

The river was diverted for defence purposes; later it was adapted to form the Mill Leet.

formed Bury St Edmunds and district) since the time of the Gloucesters the townspeople answered only to the king's itinerant justices and paid no due to The Hundred. Officially Sudbury also formed part of the Liberty of St Edmund and yet the mighty abbot seems to have had very little jurisdiction over the town.

Amicia died in 1223 and her son, Gilbert, became Earl of Gloucester and Hertford and inherited her estates but survived his mother by only seven years. It was his son, Richard de Clare, who conveyed to the burgesses by charter the pastures of Portmanscroft and King's Marsh in return for the sum of 100s paid down and an annual rent of forty shillings. This charter is undated but it formalizes the right, which the burgesses had freely held until then, to graze their cattle outside the ditch.

A second Gilbert de Clare, known as 'The Red' because of his colouring, inherited the vast Clare estates in 1262. He was a strong supporter of Simon de Montford initially but broke with him in May 1265, he was still only twenty-two. He thought he could exercise an independent role in the politics of the time but soon realised he was mistaken and outwardly at least he remained loyal to Edward I.

He obtained a divorce from his first wife in 1271 and nineteen years later, at the age of forty-seven, he married Edward's sister Joan of Acre. There was a stipulation however, the inheritance of his huge estates was henceforth restricted to the descendents of this union. This guaranteed that Sudbury would eventually revert back to the Crown.

Ten years into his inheritance, in 1272, he issued a deed of confirmation to the Burgesses and Commonalty of Sudbury of '...all the liberties and good customs that were obtained and prevailed in the days of our ancestors. To have and to hold of us and our heirs by them and their successors as freely and completely without any diminution as they and their predecessors obtained them from us and our ancestors...' None of the liberties or customs is detailed but the implication is that Sudbury people were gradually gaining more control of their town from their overlords.

The Dominican Priory

In that same year he approved and encouraged the settlement of the Dominican friars in Sudbury. The priory was founded by Baldwin de Shimperling and Chabilla his wife and set within five acres of rich pasture in the parish of All Saints. The site was on ground that had been outside the Great Ditch which was now filled in at this point. In 1352 they would be given an additional 8.5 acres by Nigel Theobald, the father of Simon of Sudbury, which formed quite a sizeable chunk of medieval Sudbury. The estate stretched from Church Street to Quay Lane and from the ditch – now Friar Street – to the river. In due course a 10ft high wall separated the friars from the townsfolk along the newly formed street and it was pierced by two gateways. One would give access to the priory house and gardens and the other to the priory church.

At this early stage the conventional buildings would have been timber framed but the church, like the others in the town, would have been constructed with flint and imported stone from the Midlands. From the start their church became a fashionable burial place for many of the surrounding gentry. The plan of the church would have been that of all the Dominican churches in England, a plain aisled hall with no division between nave and chancel. We know it had a belfry tower because it is listed in the grant to Thomas Eden at the dissolution in the sixteenth century.

Kirby's engraving of the Priory House as it was in 1748. His notes are not accurate, Sudbury friars were always of the order of St Dominic and the church was dedicated to Our Saviour and St Dominic. All that has survived from this view are the forecourt walls and their doorways.

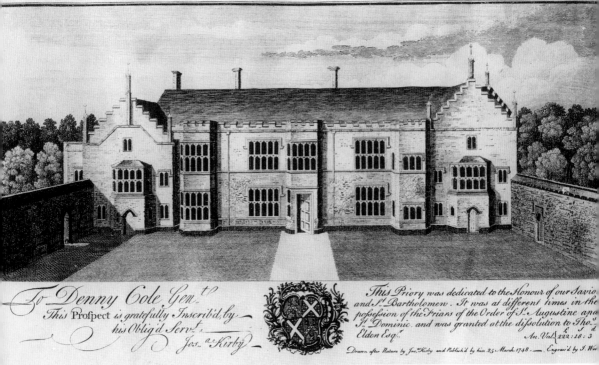

THE NORTH WEST VIEW OF SUDBURY PRIORY, IN THE COUNTY OF SUFFOLK.

To Denny Cole Gen.ᵗ

This Prospect is gratefully Inscrib'd, by his Oblig'd Serv.ᵗ Jos.ᵃ Kirby

This Priory was dedicated to the Honour of our Saviour and S.ᵗ Bartholomew. It was at different times in the possession of the Friars of the Order of S.ᵗ Augustine and S.ᵗ Dominic. and was granted at the dissolution to Tho.ˢ Elden Esq.ʳ An. Val. £222 : 18 : 3

Drawn after Nature by Jos.ᵃ Kirby and Publish'd by him 25 March 1748. — Engrav'd by J. Wo

A door from the Priory House now at No. 31 Friar's Street.

The priory became a place of considerable repute and was twice the venue for the Chapter of the Dominicans in 1316 and 1368. On both occasions the king sent a donation towards the cost of entertaining. They were also given 100 shillings from the executors of Queen Eleanor in 1291.

In 1380 they were granted a piece of land against Ballingdon Hall, 20ft square containing a spring. The gift was from Simon of Sudbury who had acquired the Manor of Ballingdon for his college. With this tiny piece of land they were granted a licence from Richard II for:

> …a certain subterraneous aqueduct from the aforesaid spring into the house of the aforesaid Prior and Friars of Sudbury, for the bringing of water from the said spring to the said house, through the King's highway and the common river of Sudbury.

The aqueduct took the form of a pear-shaped lead pipe and fragments have been discovered from time to time. The construction must have met with some opposition because Richard commanded protection:

> …for themselves and their servants etc., All Sherriffs, Mayors, Bailiffs… and etc. are charged to defend the friars and prevent molestation and…violence.

The spring still produces clear fresh water in the grounds of Ballingdon Hall above the town but not much else has survived from the Priory House. Two forecourt walls of flint with one containing a doorway and there is a fragment of the boundary wall against the street. The most important survival is the fifteenth century Priory Gate.

The Priory Gate is a rare and fine example of a medieval timber-framed monastic gatehouse. Its remarkable state of preservation is due to the fact that for many years it was hidden behind a later façade of brick and plaster and only rediscovered in the 1930s. The timber frame is now completely exposed leaving no doubt about the original function of the building. Both pedestrian and carriage entrances are exposed although the latter has been filled in leaving its timber arch with carved foliage still visible. The arch of the pedestrian doorway has been renewed but its framework and overdoor panels are original. The upper floor projects and is supported by brackets and slender shafts and all of the work can be dated to around 1450.

The Gatehouse forms part of a private residence and has been skilfully adapted with the entire structure independently exposed within. The carriage entrance is now an interesting room with both exit and entrance arches revealed. The porter's room survives intact alongside as do the two chambers upstairs with original window surrounds at the rear with grooves in their sills for wooden shutters. Altogether a remarkable survival and very well cared for. The houses opposite are mostly contemporary with this building and they stand well back to allow for the carriage sweep into the gatehouse.

A few yards past the gatehouse is a building constructed against part of the boundary wall and known until recently as The Ship and Star Inn. Originally it

had no windows on to the street, only a doorway, which inspired its earlier name as The Hole in the Wall. This house predates the Gatehouse and was most probably used by the friars as a guest house for travellers.

The Priory was dissolved by Henry VIII in 1539 and the entire estate granted to Sir Thomas Eden, a lawyer and clerk to the Star Chamber, and Griselda his wife, daughter of Sir Edward Waldegrave, whose house was nearby in Church Street. Eden wasted no time in demolishing the church which must have shocked the townspeople and the relatives of those buried within its walls. The Priory House was adapted for his own use and we are fortunate in having an engraving of it as it survived in the mid-eighteenth century.

The demolition of the house by Sir James Marriott of Twinstead Hall in 1820 was a tragedy and unnecessary. The materials were to be used in the construction of a new church at Twinstead but the designs did not meet with the approval of the bishop who made it quite clear that he would refuse to consecrate it. Sir James halted work on the structure and for some years it stood as a folly until it was demolished and the materials scattered about the neighbourhood in 1860. A fourteenth-century window from the priory found its way into the garden of a house called The Friars in Friar Street where it can still be seen.

The construction of a silk factory in the nineteenth century led to the discovery of some stone coffins and another containing a skeleton was discovered close by in the early twentieth century helping to identify the site of the church. Part of it was exposed during a minor excavation in the 1970s but no serious attempts

The fifteenth-century Priory Gatehouse. This was the gate to the Priory House and is a rare survival. The doorway was for pedestrians, the greater arch for carriages and processions. The ground floor room on the right was the porters lodging, the upper chambers were lodgings for visitors in the care of the porter.

A skeleton discovered on the priory church site in 1922.

have been made to excavate the site, much of which has now been covered by the Blackfriars development.

During the rebuilding of Ballingdon Bridge in 1902/03 a fair quantity of old stone was recovered from previous bridges on the site. Amongst it was some re-used stone from the Midlands which may well have come from the priory site to repair the bridge in the sixteenth century when it was seriously damaged. The site of the priory church being a mere 100 yards or so downstream with a pile of masonry waiting to be used would have been most convenient.

A more substantial remnant of the church, the roof of its chancel, can be seen in all its glory at Saffron Walden church in Essex. It was taken there by John Hodgkin, a friar from Sudbury, who was appointed to the vicarage at Walden in 1541. This man was a Doctor of Divinity from Cambridge who taught theology at Sudbury Priory. In 1529 he was granted the use of a house and garden to the west of the church with stabling for fifteen shillings per annum. This was probably in Church Street facing All Saints churchyard.

In 1537 he was created Bishop of Bedford but continued to reside in Sudbury until his move to Walden after the dissolution of the priory. An account of his life, which sounds very like that of the Vicar of Bray, can be found in the *Victoria County History of Suffolk*.

He was living in the shadow of the priory church when Eden set about demolishing it. He was aware that the church to which he had been appointed required a roof for its chancel and all he had to do was to persuade his patron Chancellor Audley to meet the cost, which presumably he did. For some time the church guide at Saffron Walden claimed that the roof came from St Gregory's church which was clearly not correct as all the roofs there are original and intact.

The list of important local gentry buried within the church is quite extensive according to Weaver's *Funeral Monuments* and among them was Henry, father of Robert de St Quintin, and Philip St Quintin. This family, which originated from the town of that name in France, were resident in Sudbury and were merchant traders. An inquisition held at Sudbury in 1276 claimed that Robert and John de St Quintin and seven others, all described as merchants of Amiens, were then engaged in the export of wool from Sudbury to the Continent through the port of Ipswich, '...contrary to the inhibition and forbiddance of the late and present Kings'.

The siting of St Peter's church and the wide open spaces surrounding it was a deliberate and successful piece of fourteenth-century town planning. Here is clearly seen Old Market Place on the left, Borehamgate above and Market Hill to the right.

Prior Cotton, the last Prior, was given a pension and a house opposite the Priory, now No. 62 Friar's Street.

The Market Hill, probably meant to be the site of the two annual fairs until the town was given The Croft. This 1920s view shows how the shops had narrow frontages to this valuable trading area with long extensions to the rear. The ancient entry into the Saxon town, now Gainsborough Street is at the bottom.

Robert's wife is buried in St Gregory's church under an incised tombstone showing the full-length figure of a woman with an inscription which, translated, reads:

Here lies Seive de St Quintin formerly the wife of Robert de St Quintin who died in the year of Grace 1300 on the day of St Gregory. Pray for her soul.

By 1282 the same family were exporting Sudbury cloth through Ipswich. Eight years later the name Tebaud appears as the operator of a fulling mill. Tebaud is an early spelling of the name Theobald, a family who were to prosper and have a considerable affect on the town's development.

chapter three

Fourteenth-century expansion

The de Clare family became extinct in the male line with the death of Gilbert de Clare at the battle of Bannockburn in 1314 at the age of just twenty-two. He never married and his Suffolk estates passed to his sister and co-heir Elizabeth de Burgh. Both of them were grandchildren of Edward I. Elizabeth was married and widowed three times, first to John de Burgh, Earl of Ulster who died in1313, then Theobald de Verdon who died in 1316 and finally to Roger d'Amory who died in 1322.

Each marriage produced one child, a son for the Earl of Ulster and a daughter each for the others. In 1322, at the age of twenty-seven, she was at last allowed to enjoy her own life and estates. She was an extremely wealthy woman with an estimated disposable annual income of £3,000, a huge sum in those days.

Her estates were The Honour of Clare in Suffolk, which included the manor and town of Sudbury, The Lordship of Usk in Gwent, The Cranborne Estate in Dorset, and her third share of the Clare estate in Ireland. In addition she had a jointure from John de Burgh, a dower from Theobald de Verdon and considerable land holdings from Roger d'Amory.

The estates were grouped into bailiwicks, each with its steward and reciever. There was a central finance office called The Chamber, the principal officer being Clerk of the Chamber who led a council responsible for directing her affairs. Members of her council were men who had been in Royal service including officials of the Royal Chancery and the Exchequer. Bearing in mind the stipulation concerning the Gloucester estates which governed her parent's marriage it is no wonder that the Crown was to take a close interest in the efficient running of her estates.

Amongst the archives at Westminster Abbey is a lengthy document concerning certain properties in the town dated 24 July 1318. One property in particular is described as '...a built messuage in Sudbury between the messuage

MARKET HILL, SUDBURY.

Market Hill, c. 1910. No
modern traffic and the square
is used freely by pedestrians.
Three years later
Gainsborough's statue was
unveiled in front of the church
by Princess Louise.

formerly of Thomas Warin and the lane called Stiuardeslane (Straw Lane)
abutting at one end on the street leading from the market towards the Friars
Preachers and at the other end on the said lane...' making it quite plain that the
market was still situated at the junction of Gregory Street and Stour Street.

Shortly afterwards a new and spacious market place came into being immediately outside the old East Gate. Associated with it were the thoroughfares of
North Street and Borehamgate. It was an interesting and deliberate piece of
town planning which had as a focal point a new site for a rebuilt chapel of St
Peter. Old maps and photographs taken from the air show conclusively that the
properties flanking the market place had narrow frontages with long extensions
to the rear. Eventually they would merge and become larger units behind new
façades.

The new development would provide ample funds for Elizabeth's lavish life-
style. Certainly there was a huge demand for the sites and several people
moved there from the old market and took their houses with them. Others no
doubt purchased timber for their new houses from the extensive woodlands
belonging to the manor at Woodhall.

There is clear architectural evidence in St Peter's church that building began
on the chancel around 1327 for the clerestory windows and the chancel arch
are in the Decorated style of that period. This section of the chancel and the
base of the west tower also contain several fragments of carved Norman
chevron moulding salvaged from the demolished old chapel. Work then came
to an abrupt halt and when it was resumed the new Perpendicular style was
adopted. By then other buildings were abutting the site causing severe restrictions on later enlargements.

Confirmation that the new market place was well established by 1357 is found in a document of that date referring to a piece of land called 'Leketoncroft' '...lying between the churchyard of St Gregory on one side and the road leading from the market place to the Stour on the other side.' This piece of land, now known as The Croft, would be conveyed to the town in 1393. It is interesting to note that members of a Sudbury family called Lichetun, Liketun, or Lyketon are witnesses to documents relating to St Bartholomew's Priory in the early to mid-thirteenth century. It is also possible that part of the original Leketoncroft has become separated and has survived as Acton Green (Leketon Green) just a few yards from The Croft.

Wood Hall manor house, built in 1710 on the site of the Earl of Gloucester's moated manor of Woodhall. This house was severely damaged when a plane from the nearby Chilton airbase hit the roof killing the farmer's son. The house was patched up for a while but was eventually demolished.

The number of stalls on the old market in 1314 was eighty in total. By 1340 this had increased to 102 with a larger market place. It has been claimed that a drop to only sixty-two in 1425 was a consequence of the Black Death but it was probably due more to the increase of permanent shops. It is almost certain that the sudden suspension of work on the new church was due to the plague which hit the country in 1348-49.

Amongst the most frequently quoted statistics concerning the Black Death in England are those relating to Little Cornard where fifty-one peasants died and twenty-nine families were wiped out. However, we look in vain for details concerning Sudbury and we can only assume that like most of the country it lost about a third of its population over the two years.

Elizabeth de Burgh died in 1360 having outlived her son William, Earl of Ulster, who died in 1333. Her heiress was her grand-daughter and namesake

Elizabeth de Burgh who was married to Lionel, Duke of Clarence, third son of Edward III.

The Theobald Family and Simon of Sudbury

There were several merchants in the town connected with the wool and cloth trade and amongst the most prominent were the Thebauds or Theobalds as they were later known.

William Thebaud is recorded operating a fulling mill in 1290, which he may or may not have been renting from the manor. Four years later he is mentioned in a deed renting tenteryards and a barn at the Tenterfield in Stourhallestret (Stour Street). The tenterfield, where wool was stretched on tenter hooks to dry after fulling, was situated on the site of Kentish Lodge in Stour Street, opposite The Chantry, and reached back to Walnuttree Lane. The same deed tells us that William, who is the first of the Theobalds we hear of, also owned a barn in the vicinity which is an indication that he was prospering.

This property then passed into the hands of Nigel Theobald who was most probably William's son and was also a successful merchant. He was married to Sarah according to a property conveyance in the Suffolk Record Office dated 1340. The conveyance covers the transfer of a cottage with a barn and adjacent curtilage with two pieces of land, all of it next to the land of John de Chilton and abutting upon Rotouristret (Walnuttree Lane). One piece of land lying next that of John de Wyuesle, the other piece lying between the land of Nigel Thebaud on both sides. The transfer is from Hugh de Dedham of Sudbury to Simon, son of Nigel Thebaud and Sarah, wife of Nigel.

In 1343 Nigel was providing cloth and furs for Elizabeth de Burgh and was part of her entourage at Clare Castle. He had three sons, Simon, John and Robert. Simon was destined for a career in the church, Robert seems to have been in charge of the business at Ipswich from whence he was shipping wheat in 1366, while John spent time in London and Sudbury and he appears to have been Nigel's right-hand man.

Five years after the conveyance mentioned above a quitclaim appears in the Westminster archives. A quitclaim has been described as, 'the title deed by which lawyers endeavoured to close every loophole to any subsequent claim to a property by the grantor or by his heirs and assigns'. The quitclaim at Westminster is 'from Mr Simon, son of Nigel Thebaud of Sudbury, to Nigel Thebaud, Sarah his wife, and Nigel's heirs, of all lands and tenements which he had by gift from Nigel his father in the vils of Sudbury and Melford. Given at Sudbury, 6 December 1345.' (I interpret this as a document showing Simon returning lands, which his father had given him, back to his father.)

On 4 May 1349, at the height of the Black Death in this country, another Westminster document acknowledges gifts and largesses bestowed on St Bartholomew's Priory by Elizabeth de Burgh, Nigel Thebaud and Sarah his wife, Mr Simon Thebaud, Robert Thebaud and John Thebaud. In return for which, apart from all the spiritual benefits to be obtained in the Abbey [Westminster], a daily mass would be said for each of them at St Bartholomew's by a monk at the house. Upon news of their deaths each would have a special mass as for a brother of the house, etc.

Here then, we have the entire family and their patroness, the Lady of Clare, being assured that, should they fall victim to the plague, their souls would be taken care of by the grateful Benedictines. However, two weeks later on 19 May, Nigel sets in motion a series of transactions which will culminate in St Bartholomews Priory being granted eighty acres of land and meadow in the hamlet of Holgate in Sudbury to found a chantry, 'and to celebrate therein for the souls of the above Nigel, his parents and kindred for ever...' in 1357. The necessary licence in mortmain, i.e. permission to give land to the church, was granted on 1 May 1361, the year in which Simon was made Bishop of London.

The Priory of St Bartholomew

The founding of the Chantry within the priory was probably the best thing that had ever happened at St Bartholomew's since its foundation in the twelfth century. It was only ever a small cell accommodating a prior and two monks with their servants throughout its history. From the earliest times the buildings had been timber-framed with a disastrous fire which destroyed everything in the early thirteenth century. It appears that the priory owned seventy-six acres of land and three-and-a-half acres of meadow in Sudbury by the mid-fourteenth

St Bartholomew's priory chapel, viewed from the east, built in the fourteenth century with flint and some dressed stone with typical diagonal buttresses at the corners. Until the nineteenth century, while Westminster Abbey owned it, a yearly service was held in the chapel which ensured its preservation. It was then used as a barn though kept in good repair.

century. They also owned property at Acton, Chedburgh, Clare, Kedington, Long Melford, Sturmer and Thorpe Morieux, all small amounts.

There is a copy of an indulgence from Pope Urban V (1362-70) with the following preamble, 'In view of the insufficient means of the priory of St Bartholomew, in which, it is said, are many relics of the saints, to support its burdens, and in order to encourage the alms of the faithful…'. There then follows an extraordinary list of indulgences. How much the priory gained from the Pope's gesture is unknown but combined with the Theobald Chantry there were sufficient funds to rebuild their chapel in flint and stone. It still stands complete with its original roof and is one of two monastic churches in Suffolk to have survived more or less intact, the other is at Rumburgh. It is built in the Perpendicular style without aisles and with no division between nave and chancel. The dimensions are 53ft long and 19ft wide, the height of the side walls is 17ft but 30ft to the ridge. The roof is constructed from sweet chestnut with a deliberate incline to the west to withstand the prevailing winds on the elevated site. It is a single frame or wagon-type roof with the area above the altar boarded and once painted. In the east wall are two niches which once held statues and there is a piscina set in the south wall by a blocked doorway. The two windows on either side of the chapel have lost their tracery, unless it is hidden behind the plaster but the original south doorway and door have survived. There are indications that a side chapel or vestry may have stood on the south side but it may have been a cloister linking the chapel to the priory house.

It has always been said that the priory house was demolished in 1779 but recent investigations seem to indicate that substantial parts have survived beneath the present farmhouse. The magnificent timber-framed and weather-boarded barn has been dated to the fourteenth century. It has six aisled bays with two wagon entrances on the south side and the roof is thatched with Norfolk reed.

Both Nigel and Sarah had died before 1365 but the chapel was not completed in time to receive their bodies. They were buried instead at St Gregory's church where Simon built a small chapel for them dedicated to All Souls. This may have been the reason for the abbey's decision to transfer the priory and all its possessions to Simon's newly founded college attached to St Gregory's in exchange for a messuage and three shops in the city of London. The licence for the transfer was obtained in 1380 and a deed was drawn up in 1382, the year after Simon's death. It was accompanied by an extremely detailed inventory listing every single item at the priory so that we know what each room contained and how the chapel was furnished. It is a strangely haunting and moving document.

The chapel contained three 6ft benches and three 8ft benches, one very strong chest for vestments, one portable altar, two bronze candlesticks, various books, altar cloths and two red chasubles etc., one gilt cross. Of relics they had one part of the arm of St Bartholomew and one strand of the hair of St Mary.

above The chapel from the south, a few yards from the farmhouse which incorporates much of the original priory house.

left The priory barn is a magnificent fourteenth-century structure. As the priory was run by monks of senior years from Westminster it is calculated that some seventy or so are buried on this site.

For reasons unknown to us the exchange never took place. The priory remained a cell of Westminster and was used as a posting for monks about to retire so there may be more graves than previously thought. The abbey closed down the priory and leased the property out to William Butt of London in 1536. When the abbey ceased to be a monastery and was refounded as The collegiate church of St Peter at Westminster by Henry VIII, the priory was returned to them as part of their endowment. They continued to lease it out as a farm with the chapel set aside for worship and paid the stipend for a curate. They disposed of the property in the nineteenth century when the chapel became a barn.

The Hospital of St Leonard – Colney's Hospital

John Colney was a prosperous merchant in Sudbury who had the misfortune to succumb to leprosy. Such unfortunates were compelled by law to withdraw from society and live apart or with fellow sufferers outside the town. Being a man of substance he founded and endowed a small hospital consisting of three self-contained tenements one of which he occupied and became the hospital's first governor. The hospital was situated outside the town on the road to Melford and St Edmundsbury at the foot of St Bartholomew's Lane.

The endowment of the hospital consisted of the house and garden and five acres of land which included a vineyard on the opposite side of the road against Brundon Lane. This was conveyed to the Freemen in 1895 as part of their common land and was annexed to North Meadows.

John Colney approached Simon Theobald, who was now Bishop of London, to draw up certain ordinances for the control and governing of the hospital and this was done in 1372. The hospital was to accommodate three lepers, one of whom (Colney himself) would be governor. After Colney's death the vacancy would be filled and one would be chosen as governor to whom the others would obey. If a leper died, was expelled or resigned, a replacement was to be found within six months, failing which the spiritual father of St Gregory's should nominate a third.

The annual income was to be divided into five portions, two to the governor, two to the brethren and one for maintenance. This fifth portion was to be kept with the writings of the house in a common chest in some church or safe place in Sudbury. The governor was to hold one key and the other was to be with a person deputed by the mayor of Sudbury. If the statutes should not be duly kept after the founder's death the revenues were to be divided between the church of St Gregory and the chapel of St Anne, annexed to the same in equal portions for the souls of Colney, the founder, and of Nigel and Sarah Theobald and all the faithful departed.

The estates of the hospital were vested in feoffees by deed of 16 January 1445. From then it is frequently mentioned in the Corporation Books as 'The Little House at the Colnes'. The hospital was rebuilt in 1619/20 as three almshouses but the residents were still obliged to swear to the original oath upon admittance:

> You shall swear that you will well and truly observe all the ancient rules and orders of this house (as Governor or fellow of the same) so long as you shall continue therein, according to the utmost of your skill and knowledge; you shall be obedient to the members thereof as your state does require in all things lawfull; you shall quietly submit to all such deprivation and expulsion as by competent authority shall be inflicted on you, for such crimes and misdemenours as they shall judge worthy of the same; and all other rules and orders which shall hereafter be made by sufficient authority for the due governance and regulation of the said hospital you peaceably acquiesce in – So help you God.

The hospital seemed to work well under Simon's statutes until the last resident and master of the hospital, Mr Loveday, died in 1813. Eventually in 1867 the net income was applied towards the support of St Leonards Cottage Hospital in Newton Road, via the Charity Commisioners. St Leonard was the Patron Saint of Lepers.

Nothing has survived of the seventeenth-century building because it was demolished in 1858 and replaced with a pair of detached double tenements, which still stand on the site today, at a cost of £376.

Simon Theobald's College of St Gregory

Simon's career culminated in his reaching the highest position in the church in England but it was to lead to his downfall and death. He was born around 1318 with the proverbial silver spoon in his mouth, his father being a wealthy man, buying and selling large quantities of wool and cloth, according to the Calenders of Close Rolls 1330-45. He was one of the new mercantile class on whom King Edward III depended to help finance the first campaign of what was to become the Hundred Years War. Nigel Theobald was loaning sums equivalent to £15-20,000 today.

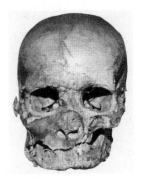

The head of Simon of Sudbury, Archbishop of Canterbury and Chancellor of England. Beheaded by the mob in The Peasants' Revolt his body was taken to Canterbury where it is buried next to the Black Prince in the choir of the cathedral. His head was brought back to the college and was probably regarded as part of the fixtures and fittings. It was handed over to St Gregory's church in the eighteenth century or possibly earlier.

Simon was sent to study at Paris University, before the hostilities of 1336-37, where he was awarded a Doctorate of Civil Law. He was engaged in diplomatic missions for the king and we have to consider at least whether his father's close contacts with Elizabeth De Burgh had anything to do with that. He also became chaplain to the Pope and acted as a Papal Nunceo. In 1349 he was made a canon at Hereford and four years later canon at Salisbury. He was created Bishop of London in 1361 but was not enthroned until a year later.

He was now beginning to acquire considerable wealth by investing in commercial property in the city. The substantial revenues of his Bishopric enabled him to become a public benefactor. Unlike monks at that time he was not subject to any vow of poverty. He was of course subject to a vow of celibacy which meant that there would be no family to support. John Harvey, one of our finest experts on medieval architecture and craftsmen, has dated the north aisle of St Gregory's church to around 1360-70 and one of the roof bosses depicts the Talbot or Hound of the Theobalds. Certainly the most eastern bay, built to house the tomb of his parents, was completed in 1365.

The first indication of his plans to raise the church to collegiate status was recorded 1374 when he exchanged four of the shops he had bought in Fish Street, London for the advowson of St Gregory's church from the nuns at Eaton in Warwickshire who had been given it by the Earl of Gloucester in the mid-twelfth century. In 1375 he was made Archbishop of Canterbury and in that year the first deed was drawn up for the founding of a college for the training of priests between Simon, his brother John, and the Bishop of Norwich whose diocese Sudbury was in. His motivation for founding such an institution was the current appalling state of the priesthood where a large percentage were

This engraving shows the remains of the College of St Gregory as they were when it was being used as a workhouse in the 1820s. It was demolished finally to make way for a new workhouse in 1835/6

ignorant of Latin and had little idea of what they were actually saying when reciting the liturgy.

The college was built on the site of his father's house and on a piece of adjoining land which Simon had purchased in 1340. As his father's house would have been quite substantial the chances are that much of it was incorporated within the new building which commenced in 1380. Interestingly, it was built with brick round a quadrangle with a hall, chapter house, library, dormitory's, and accommodation for the master. It was endowed with 570 acres of land which formed the manors of Middleton Hall and Ballingdon. A year later saw additional endowments of three shops in St Michael's parish, Cornhill, London and gifts of plate, books and furnishings.

The church was now under the jurisdiction of the college and was to undergo considerable rebuilding which would see the chancel serving as the college chapel leaving the nave and aisles for the parishioners. The chapel of St Peter on the new market place, which was awaiting completion, was also under their control and there was now good reason to finish the work. The guilds wanted a building suitable for their processions and the performance of the popular miracle plays. It should reflect the growing importance of Sudbury as a cloth town and provide a civic church independent of the college. Work recommenced immediately and explains the anomaly of two large medieval churches in one parish.

Simon's connection with the college was brought to an abrupt halt in 1381 when he was executed by the mob on Tower Hill at the height of the Peasants' Revolt. Much has been written about that rebellion and there is not space to deal with it fully here but there are certain facts worth noting and we will come to them later. It must have come as a great shock when news of his murder and the manner of his death reached Sudbury. Nothing was allowed to halt the work in progress at the college however. By 1386 the college had acquired the manor of Brundon and other lands in and around Sudbury.

Work on the remodelling of St Gregory's, which had been started by Simon, continued, so that between 1385 and 1450 they had raised the nave roof by adding a clerestory and rebuilt the south aisle, St Anne's Chapel, and the porch It was now ready for the crowning achievement, the rebuilding of the chancel to form the college chapel for the master (or Custos), five secular canons, three chaplains, and the choristers for their exclusive use. It would be built in the latest Perpendicular style and the parishioners would be given a new altar at the east end of the nave. But that would all be in the next century.

The Peasants' Revolt and Sudbury

Before the Black Death there had been a surplus of labour but afterwards it was drastically reduced. As a consequence the fuedal system began to crack as the surviving labour force began exploiting the situation. Many hirers of labour, including royal bailiffs and such great monastic houses as St Edmundsbury, who owned half of Suffolk, offered competitive wages and turned a blind eye as to

This photograph, taken in 1970, shows the centre crossroads of the early medieval town. Top right is the long curve of the ditch which became Friar's Street. Sepulchre Street, now Gainsborough Street, runs down from the top left corner to the centre where it meets Stour Street. Between Friar's Street and Gainsborough Street can be seen Wylewerlelane, (Christopher Lane) and William Wood's Grammar School.

whether they were engaging freemen or villeins escaping bondage from a neighbouring manor. Some landowners grassed their lands and began breeding sheep as the foreign demand for English cloth showed no signs of falling. The tax on the export of woollen cloth was high but the cloth merchants still made a handsome living.

The king's government of 1351 introduced the Statute of Labourers which ruled that rents and wages should be fixed in a desperate attempt to curb the situation. Similar statutes were issued by successive governments to no avail. The labourers naturally resented these attempts to keep down their wages. They had tasted the beginnings of their emancipation especially in the Stour Valley where more and more people were becoming employed in the cloth trade. They resented the threat to their new standard of living.

In other parts of the country thousands of peasants forced to return to labour services were aware of their more fortunate fellows, sometimes only a mile or so away, seeming to have more independence. This was an awakening peasantry, with a strong sense of passed wrongs, impatient and frustrated, tired of the continued wars with the French and tired of paying taxes to sustain them.

At St Edmundsbury where the whole town and most of west Suffolk came under the jurisdiction of the great Benedictine abbey, there had been several uprisings. The worst was in 1327 when they had demanded and been granted a charter after attacking the abbey, only to have it rescinded later by the sheriff and the ringleaders hanged. Now in 1381 the situation was again volatile. A new abbot had been chosen by the Pope and another by the monks, the Pope's man lying in prison for importing the papal bull. The abbey was in the temporary charge of the prior, John Cambridge, and so were the townspeople who loathed him. It was like a powder keg awaiting a lighted match.

At around this time there was also growing animosity towards the Flemings, skilled craftsmen invited into this country by Edward III to show the English what to do with their wool to make it into the finest woollen cloth in Europe. To the average Englishman the Flemish were exploiters who lived on sweated labour and sent their earnings back to Flanders. They dressed differently and kept themselves apart. In the rebellion they were to suffer terribly, many of them being dragged from their houses in London and executed in the street.

There was no single cause for the rebellion but a feeling by the population of being wronged on a number of scores. Each individual involved was certain that they knew who was responsible for their particular grievance and when the opportunity arose would seek satisfaction. The nation seemed to have lost confidence in itself. And how did poor Simon Theobald, Simon of Sudbury as he was known, become so involved? Quite simply because apart from being Archbishop of Canterbury he was also chancellor, in spite of the fact that a few years earlier Parliament had declared that 'none but laymen henceforth be made chancellor, treasurer … or other great officers of the realm'. He arranged for Parliament to assemble in November 1380 at Northampton and he explained to them the dreadful situation the nation was in financially.

The French expeditions had emptied the treasury. There had been troubles in Flanders so exports of wool were down. There were three months wages due to the garrisons of Brest, Cherbourg and Calais. The king's jewels were in pawn to the city of London as a surety for a loan of £5,000. The king needed the sum of £160,000 if they were to continue the war with France.

Since it was generally agreed that there could be no withdrawing from the war it was now up to them to raise the money. They were told that there were three choices, a sales tax on all mercantile transactions, a wealth tax on property, or a poll tax which would amount to one shilling and three groats per head on all persons over the age of fifteen.

They settled on a poll tax to raise £100,000 if the church raised the rest. There was one proviso, the richest in each district would pay up to six groats per man and wife so that the tax would fall less heavily on others. A groat was the equivalent of four pence. When the decision was reached the Lord Treasurer resigned and Sir Robert Hales, prior of the Knights Hospitalers was appointed in his place.

Parliament may have been in agreement but the nation thought differently. The rebellion that followed has been well documented elsewhere. It reached its climax with the dreadful events of 13-15 June 1381 when an estimated 100,000 peasants entered London.

On the 12 June a detachment of Essex men led by a priest, John Wrawe, came to the Essex-Suffolk border where they were joined by a few Sudbury men and with the vicar of All Saints, Geoffrey Parfrey, as their leader. They made their way to Liston Hall, two miles outside the town, the home of Richard Lyons the wealthy merchant and notorious moneylender. He was not at home but they wrecked his house and destroyed manorial and other records before moving on to Cavendish. They were in search of Chief Justice Cavendish who was responsible for enforcing the Statute of Labourers in East Anglia, he had fled but not before storing his valuables for safety in the church tower. The rebels demanded entry into the tower and carried off his goods.

From Cavendish they went to Melford but strangely made no attempt to enter Melford Hall, the country seat of the Abbot of St Edmundsbury. Instead they took refreshment at a tavern on the green owned by a man called Onewene. They paid him three shillings and fourpence for their victuals before moving on to St Edmundsbury where they learned that the hated Prior John Cambridge had been murdered by his own serfs. They ran Cavendish to ground at Lakenheath where his head was struck off and carried back to St Edmundsbury for display.

In London on Friday 14 June the boy king Richard II rode out from the Tower to meet the rebels at Mile End. After his departure nobody seems to have given the order for the drawbridge to be raised. Inside the Tower Simon and Hales the Treasurer were in the small chapel of St John hearing mass. Richard did not return to the Tower but went instead to Baynards Castle further upstream. Wat Tyler however did return and with an estimated 400 men crossed the drawbridge and entered the Tower with no resistance from the captain of the guard.

There has been much debate about this incident. Had Richard agreed to the surrender of Simon and Hales knowing what their fate would be, even though neither was responsible for the wretched state of the economy? Or was it that the guard had not been given orders to resist? It remains a mystery as no official record can be found to establish the truth.

Simon and Hales were dragged from the chapel on to Tower Green and were clumsily decapitated. Their heads were fixed on to poles and paraded to Westminster and back before being placed over the gatehouse of London Bridge, where heads of traitors were usually displayed. Eventually Simon's body was buried in the choir at Canterbury alongside that of the Black Prince. His head was somehow brought back to his college in his native town and is now housed in the vestry of St Gregory's church.

It was left to the Bishop of Norwich, Henry Despenser, who later earned a reputation as a warrior ecclesiastic, to restore order in East Anglia. It has been claimed that the last stragglers of the mob were rounded up on Market Hill and duly executed and this was given credence when a group of headless bodies was discovered against the churchyard wall on The Croft in the last century. All the promises made by the young king were broken. The leaders of the rebellion were executed including a certain John Starling from Essex who had gone marching about with a sword hanging round his neck claiming that he was the man who had killed Simon. He was hanged, drawn and quartered.

Richard, who had been crowned by Simon, showed great courage during those weeks but failed dismally as a king thereafter. He was finally deposed and died a prisoner at Pontefract at the age of thirty three. When the old chapel of St Peter in Sudbury was demolished and its materials used in the new building at the top of the hill, a large inn was built on the site to accommodate pilgrims and travelling merchants. Its sign was The White Hart, the emblem and badge of Richard II.

The Wool and Cloth Trade

During the fourteenth century English wool was in great demand on the continent, especially in Flanders where cloth-making skills were advanced. The main producers of the finest English wool were the great monastic houses in the West Country and Lincolnshire. The wool merchants in Suffolk exported the raw material and imported the hand-woven cloth through the ports of Ipswich and Lynn. English cloth was below the continental standard and it was because of this that Edward III invited the Flemish weavers in against much local disapproval. He was therefore obliged to guarantee their protection although his successor Richard II failed miserably to honour it during the Peasants' Revolt.

As the cloth-making trade developed it was strictly controlled by the trade guilds. English-woven woollen cloth became the finest in Europe The trade guilds saw that standards of quality were maintained and regulated the trade, making sure that their members were protected from outside competition. Eventually the wool brokers found the guild restrictions were stifling and in an attempt to gain more freedom from their control began employing large forces of direct labour in the villages away from the towns. From now on the brokers became known as clothiers and the Stour Valley became the scene of an intensive and efficient industry which would bring great wealth into the area.

The most important necessity for producing the cloth was flowing water and there was plenty of it in the valley with its tributary streams and subsidiary valleys of the Glem, Box, Chad and Brett. The water was essential for fulling which was just one of at least six procedures which the wool went through, briefly they were as follows:

1　Sorting: sorting, washing and scouring the wool and soaking in oil.
2　Carding: mixing the short wool fibres together on spiked boards.
3　Spinning: twisting wool for cohesion and making into packs of yarn.
4　Weaving: into cloth.
5　Fulling: thickening the cloth by beating and scouring in water and scrubbing with Fuller's Earth (Aluminium Oxide) to remove excess oil. Originally cloth was trodden underfoot by a 'walker' but by 1250 a wooden bar beater operated by water power was introduced (fulling mill). After fulling the cloth was stretched on large frames known as 'tenters' to dry (hence tenter hooks and tenter fields, as in Stourhallestrete).
6　Dyeing and Finishing: although wool was often dyed before carding and spinning.

Dyeing was a delicate and expensive procedure and was often sub-contracted out. Large quantities of dye were needed often amounting to twice the weight of cloth to be dyed. Most of the cheaper colours were made from local vegetation, e.g. green and yellow from onions, nettles and cow parsley: blue and purple from elderberries, damsons and sloes: red from sorrel and lady's bedstraw: black and grey from alder bark and yellow iris: magenta from dandelion. Saffron was made from the saffron crocus grown on the Saffron Field (now Belle Vue). Other richer colours such as scarlet and vermilion had to be imported.

Woad was used to colour the famous Sudbury Broadcloths and Narrow Cloths and this was imported from Spain. It came in dry balls which had to be ground and mixed with water and left to ferment. Much of the vegetation used by the dyers can still be found growing in the hedgerows outside Sudbury today. Likewise, there are families in the district bearing names which have come down from the trade such as Dyer, Fuller, Weaver and Cardy, or Corder, and Walker.

One man could work the loom for the Sudbury Narrows but it took two men to throw the shuttle for the broadcloths which were 24 yards in length.

chapter four

Fifteenth century: the glory years

There is ample evidence of the prosperity which the cloth trade brought to Sudbury to be seen in the many buildings which have survived from that era. Throughout East Anglia it is chiefly seen through the rebuilding on a grand scale of the parish churches and Sudbury is no exception. Although each of them retains part of its fourteenth-century fabric they are for the greater part fifteenth-century buildings in the new and fashionable Perpendicular style. The wealthy and pious citizens of this now prosperous town produced three remarkable and beautiful churches and furnished them accordingly.

Because of the lack of building stone in this region the churches are mainly constructed from flint and reused material from earlier buildings. For example, examination of the walls of the tower at St Peter's will show reused, worked Norman stone from the old chapel which stood at the foot of the hill. Even more rewarding will be a close study of the second stage of the tower at St Gregory's where large clusters of reused Saxon bricks have recently been identified by Peter Minter and Dr John Potter who are experts in the field of brickwork. Here also can be seen Roman and early medieval bricks and tiles from buildings which stood in the vicinity with much dressed stone from the earlier churches on the site. The walls of All Saints in Church Street are no less interesting.

All secular buildings were timber framed and some fourteenth-century structures have survived in part, more than was previously thought, but the bulk of them have their origins in the fifteenth century. Many complete houses have survived from this era and there are far more in Sudbury than is apparent because later centuries have seen them encased in brick. A good example to which the public has access is Gainsborough's House, at No. 46 Gainsborough Street where two timber-framed houses of differing dates are hidden behind an eighteenth-century brick façade.

There were many variations of the timber-framed house, the most common having a central main hall with one, or sometimes two, cross wings. Another

type was the long narrow dwelling with a gabled front to the street and interconnecting rooms towards the rear, although sometimes a corridor ran along the side. The front was used as a shop with workshops and stores to the rear and living quarters on the first floor. This is the type which once lined the Market Hill but the two finest surviving examples were demolished in the 1960s, Page's ironmongers and Flack's cycle shop next to the Black Boy, though both had been hidden behind later façades.

Such houses were prefabricated in the joiner's yard where each timber was marked according to its position then dismantled and re-erected on the chosen site. Space between the timbers was filled with a mixture of mud and sticks known as 'wattle and daub' which was then plastered over. These houses were just as easily dismantled and moved to other parts of the town and extended or reduced in size according to the owner's requirements, leaving interesting puzzles for later historians.

External plastering of the walls was often enhanced with decorative relief moulding known as pargetting but only fragmentary pieces have survived in Sudbury. One has to visit Hadleigh, Clare or Lavenham to see good local examples although the very finest is probably the seventeenth-century work on the Ancient House at Ipswich.

The earliest type of roofing was thatch but there is good reason to believe that small tiles were becoming the norm in Sudbury at quite an early date. Large quantities are reused in the walls of the churches and there is an early reference

The Old Moot Hall in Cross Street. It began as a house built in the late fourteenth century but was used for civic purposes from the start. A new Moot Hall was built in the sixteenth century on the Market Hill but a huge painting of the arms of James I on the chimney breast in the lower chamber suggests that this was still being used for official business.

dated 1386 at Bury Record Office amongst the papers concerning St Saviour's Hospital at St Edmundsbury, thus, 'paid sixpence for a messenger to go to Clare and on to Sudbury for tiles for the pavement of St Thomas's Chapel'. There is terracotta work from this period inside St Gregory's which points to a brick and tile industry functioning at Sudbury at a much earlier date than has hitherto been suspected.

There were some excellent carpenters working in Sudbury at this time and we have the names of some of them. For example John Golding from Sudbury was contracted by the Duke of York in 1450 to build the floodgates at the mill and other work at Clare Castle. Thomas Gooch, also from Sudbury, was contracted to make the rood screen and loft at Clare church in 1478. We may surmise that he may well have been responsible for some of the excellent screen work in St Peter's and All Saints in the town. His will was proved in 1483 and he was survived by a son who was also a carpenter who adopted the name of Carver and took up residence in St Gregory's College.

As a resident carpenter at the college Thomas Carver becomes a candidate for the work on the chancel at St Gregory's under the direction of the master, William Wood (c. 1461-91). Carver's will was proved in 1510.

The most famous of all was Thomas Loveday who was born in Sudbury and grew up to become one of the twenty-four burgesses of the town. Towards the end of the fifteenth century he was already a recognised craftsman and was involved in the sale of two properties to Robert Fynch of Bulmer. In the period 1505-10 there is a wealth of documentation showing him in charge of the

This splendid range in Stour Street contains merchant's houses of about 1450 but includes part of an earlier building at the centre.

Stour Hall, now called Cleeve Hall and the site of Sudbury Manor, was built in around 1450 and once had gables. These were replaced with a hipped roof in the eighteenth century.

building of Little Saxham Hall for the Solicitor General, Thomas Lucas. He was sent by Lucas to visit the house of Angel Donne in Tower Street, London, which had a belvedere tower of brick.

In 1516 and still living in Sudbury he secured the contract for much of the woodwork at St John's College in Cambridge. He was contracted to supply the chapel stalls, the rood loft and screen, three pairs of gates, ten doors, the lantern of the stair turret of the gate tower, the floors of the chambers and the desks for the library. Most important of all was the roof of the hall for this was his speciality.

Loveday's roofs are rich and varied and they can be seen in the vicinity of Sudbury. The finest are the hammer beam roofs at Gestingthorpe (1524) and Castle Hedingham (1530) and the chancel roof at Bulmer. Lavenham Guildhall (1529-30) has been attributed to him probably through the Oxford connections at Hedingham. He died and was buried at Castle Hedingham in 1536. He was a close friend of Simon Clerk the master mason at Kings College and probably Lavenham church.

The finest fifteenth-century timber-framed buildings in Sudbury can match anything of their kind elsewhere and include the Salter's Hall range in Stour Street, The Priory Gate in Friar's Street and Stour Hall (now named Cleeve Hall) in Stour Street. There were many more of course long since demolished or concealed behind later work which we will consider later. Sudbury people though are also justly proud of three medieval churches which dominate the old town and we will look at them now in some detail, beginning with the earliest foundation, St Gregory's.

The fifteenth-century carved south doors in the porch of St Gregory's were once enriched with the figures of six saints.

St Gregory's Church

This is very much the 'Mother Church' of Sudbury with a history stretching back to the earliest days of Christianity in this area. It is generally supposed to have existed some years before Bishop Alfhun's visit in 797 and subsequent bequests dated 970 and 993 seem to suggest that this was a Minster church serving an area much greater than Sudbury. It stands above the banks of the diverted river on the edge of the tree-shaded Croft in the northernmost corner of the Iron Age defences.

There have been at least four churches on this site and the first may well have been a humble timber structure but the recent identification of Saxon bricks reused in the tower indicates a pre-Norman rebuild. We know it was rebuilt in the fourteenth century because the pillars of the nave arcade have survived. The church as we see it now represents a complete remodelling begun on the north side in 1361 by Simon Theobald and completed by the college around 1470-75. The last addition was the plain Tudor red brick vestry built after the closure of the college in 1544.

The church exterior

A view of St Gregory's from the southeast showing the unusually deep porch.

Except for the tower and the brick vestry, and possibly the north aisle which may be fourteenth century, the rest of the fabric dates from the fifteenth century. All the windows have the depressed arch of the late Perpendicular period as at

All Saints. There is evidence inside which shows that the tower was certainly begun in the mid-fourteenth century. It has angle stepped buttresses to the east but diagonal to the west. There is a large south-east stair turret which rises above the battlements but unlike the other towers in Sudbury here they are even and not stepped and there are no pinnacles. The turret has no parapet and at the foot is an altar tomb beneath a deeply recessed arch. The tomb chest is decorated with two blank shields set in lozenges and beneath the arch is an indent for a brass which confirms that this tomb has been removed from within the church, probably when the chancel was rebuilt. Nineteenth-century reports refer to the arms of Drury being visible at one time.

Apart from the Saxon bricks already mentioned there is a large amount of reused masonry visible besides huge quantities of tiles, a few of which are Roman. On the north aisle is a broad band of flint and stone chequer-work, this was an original feature restored by Butterfield in 1862. The east and west windows of this aisle have good tracery and are the earliest in the church. A feature of great interest is the terracotta gargoyles, the earliest of this type known in England.

The south porch is unusually deep and with the adjoining chapel under one roof forms a transept. Marriage services were often conducted in the church porch, as was the service of the Churching of Women after giving birth. For this purpose a portable altar would be set up before the carved doors and because of this they are worth studying closely.

The doors have a carved trailing tracery border and there are six tracery heads beneath which are clear indications that there once existed six carved canopies. The slots for the projecting canopies remain and just beneath them are the knops which once supported six carved figures, all of which would have provided a reredos for the portable altar transforming the porch into a temporary chapel.

Interior

The first impression is that this is a well cared for church and it is full of light. One also notices the extraordinary length of the chancel which seems to dwarf the nave although both are of the same length. The arcade is of four bays only and is of the fourteenth century with the pillars being rounded beneath the arches but polygonal towards the aisles and nave with simple capitals to the rounded parts only. The windows above the arcade (the clerestory) are fifteenth century and the outline of the earlier roof can be seen above the tower arch.

The nave roof is of cambered tie beam construction with open arch bracing to the principal rafters. There is geometric open tracery carving and some nice carved bosses. The eastern bay is ceiled and panelled with ribs and bosses as a canopy of honour for a nave altar which was introduced when the chancel was rebuilt to serve as the college chapel.

At the western end of the nave stands the font, not modern as until recently thought, but probably late fourteenth century with each side of the octagonal bowl decorated with tracery panels beneath which are small carved figures

above St Gregory's interior, looking west, with Butterfield's altar rails in the foreground. Note the windows are only half glazed because the choir stalls once had tall canopied backs.

right A carved, winged beast on the return stalls of the choir.

opposite Simon's Hound, or Talbot, as a misericord decoration in the choir stalls of St Gregory's.

depicting priests heads, animal heads, a snake biting its own tail (eternity) and a crowned skull. Suspended from the roof by an iron rod above the font is its spectacular cover of around 1450, or earlier.

The cover is a brilliant construction in two stages, the first is an octagonal drum – each side forming a niche for a statue with a beautiful nodding ogee canopy and tracery carved back. Delicate flying buttresses between each niche remind one of the famous Eleanor crosses erected to the memory of Eleanor of Castile after her death in 1290. The second section is formed by a triple tier of tracery with more butresses and open canopies culminating with a tapering crocketed spire with a beautiful octagonal finial from which were suspended the veils to cover such ostentation during lent. The eight statues have vanished and never been replaced but it says much for the craftsmanship that the cover remains beautiful without them. It is 12ft tall and retains much of its original colouring and gesso work. The lower stage rises telescopically to reveal a base with more tracery carving. This is one of a group of such covers but few have survived in such excellent condition and it has been said that none other can match it for the qualities of proportion and elegance.

The elegant pulpit by Paul Earee of Sudbury has been shortened in height, it was presented by Sir Worthington Church in 1925. The decorative lamp brackets are from the Butterfield restoration of 1862.

The aisles

Of the two aisles the north aisle is the earlier and its eastern most bay, now occupied by the organ, is the burial place of Simon Theobald's parents – Sarah and Nigel Theobald. The bay formed the chapel of All Souls built by Simon in 1365 and at one time commemorated in stained glass with the following inscription:

ORATE PRO DOMINO – SIMON THEOBALD ALIAS SUDBURY QUI ISTAM CAPELLAM FUNDAVIT ANNO DOMINI 1365 – IN COMMEMORATIONE OMNIUM ANIMARUM – DEDICAT DAT CONSECRAT

There is a strong possibility that Simon paid for the complete rebuilding of this aisle during 1365-70. The timber roofs throughout the church are original and in this aisle there are three terracotta bosses, one is a wreath of oak leaves, another is the head of a green man, the third depicts the talbot or hound of the Theobald family. This was also the crest or badge of the college so it is not clear whether Simon or the college was the builder.

The south aisle is later, probably 1425-50, and tucked away in the south-east corner is the incised tomb slab of the wife of Robert St Quintin who died in 1300. This type of memorial is quite rare in this country but there is another larger and finer example in Middleton church, Essex, less than a mile from Sudbury. Close by is the tomb slab of William Wood, master of the college 1467-91. It was placed here during the Butterfield restoration, his body lies on the north side of the high altar in the chancel.

The south chapel once housed two altars, one beneath each of the two east windows. They were dedicated to St Mary and St Anne; a juxtaposition of altars often seen in medieval churches. It is believed that the shrine of Our Lady of Sudbury was housed within this chapel and was much visited by pilgrims journeying to and from St Edmundsbury. The wife of Henry VII sent 2 and 7d to this shrine in 1502 as she was not well enough to make the pilgrimage to Walsingham. It was her son who ordered its destruction some years later.

The chapel is now home to two large box tombs, one to the Pannell family who lived at the college during the seventeenth century, the other is that of

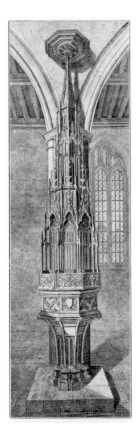

above An engraving showing the font cover at St Gregory's dated 1792 but not showing the rod from which it is suspended from the ceiling.

right Neale's engraving of St Gregory's in 1826 showing the font cover opening like a cupboard. It also shows the font in some detail but again not the rod which it must have had to suspend the cover to take the weight when the door was opened.

Thomas Carter who died in 1706. The Latin inscription on the side of the chest is translated as follows:

> Traveller, I will relate to you a wondrous thing, when the aforesaid breathed his last, a Sudbury camel passed through the eye of a needle. If thou hast wealth, go and do thou likewise.

Details of his generosity are displayed, in English this time, on a massive wall tablet. He was a clothier employing many people and his house was at No. 1 Stour Street. The money he left for the poor of Sudbury is still distributed on St Thomas's Day in the form of vouchers.

49

The Chancel

Without doubt the building of this chancel to form the college chapel was commissioned by the master of the college, William Wood, who was master from 1467 until his death in 1491. For a man who was to have a profound affect on Sudbury comparatively little is known about his origins. What we do know is based on his work as master and the contents of his will. He was wealthy and a Renaissance man; well read, pious, cultured, with exquisite taste, and concerned for the future of mankind.

Apart from being master, or custos, of the college he was also Archdeacon of Sudbury, rector of Fornham All Saints and rector of St Gregory's and St Peter's in Sudbury. It is made quite clear in his will that he was a bibliophile and a collector of Chinese porcelain which had a value higher than gold in those days when nobody in Europe knew the secrets of its manufacture. It reached Europe through the trade routes to Venice and regular trading with Italy would have brought it to England, but it was extremely scarce. At that time China was ruled by the Ming emperors.

Architectural details and style place the building of the chapel, now the chancel, in the third quarter of the fifteenth century, which fits perfectly with Wood's term as master. The length of the building is 62ft, the same as the nave, which would be unusual if its original function was not known. It is built in the refined Perpendicular style with large windows which have the minimum of stone tracery to allow for large areas of stained glass, all of which was destroyed in the seventeenth century. It was furnished with a complete set of stalls for the brethren but two of these, and the master's stall, are now missing, leaving nineteen in all.

The fact that the windows are blocked below the transom and that there are cuts in the masonry indicate that the stalls once had tall canopies above them, cathedral style. Similarly the half blocked east window points to the existence of a huge reredos behind the altar. The walls would have had painted decoration and all of this was crowned by the remarkable Renaissance style ceiling.

The flat ceiling is panelled out with moulded ribs forming geometric shapes with a beautiful cornice of scroll leaf carving and angels with spread wings. Those above the sanctuary carry instruments of the Passion, i.e. a hammer, nails, ladder, scourge, crown of thorns but the others are praying. The colouring is sadly not original and it deserves a restoration to the richer colours it once had, similar to the font cover. It is an astonishing ceiling, very Renaissance in character and the earliest of its type in England, predating others by at least forty-five years. One wonders how the design was conceived. It is possible that Wood had come across one of the books on architecture coming out of Italy at that time, or he may have been to Venice or Tuscany himself and seen such ceilings.

In his will he desires that his body be buried, 'in a certain part of the sanctuary of the collegiate church of St Gregory aforesaid, being in daily view of the master or warden and co-brethren of the present and all future times'. Burial within the sanctuary was strictly reserved for the founder, builder, or patron of the church in pre-Reformation days. It is not known why his stone was re-located in the nineteenth century.

We know from wills that there was a rood screen across the chancel arch at one time but there is no indication of an access to the rood loft. It has also recently come to light that the chancel arch was widened in 1890 though the original pillars were retained. It is my belief that William Wood removed the rood screen and replaced it with a tall pulpitum screen decorated with tiers of painted saints from which a small panel has survived depicting Sir John Schorne casting the devil from a boot signifying a cure for gout.

The nineteen stalls form the largest collection of misericords in the county. A misericord is the carved projection beneath the upturned seat and they are often worthy of study. Among these examples are some interesting human heads with contemporary headgear, some mythological creatures and the hound from the college arms. The armrests take the form of human heads but all the carving here is restrained.

An attempt to restore colour to the walls in 1885 was disastrous and it remained until 1927 when it was finally obliterated. Only the painted figures on the lower lights of the blocked windows remain from that scheme and they were painted by Aveling Green. The tiling of the floor and the altar rails are from Butterfield's restoration.

The late Tudor brick vestry to the north of the chancel does not intrude thankfully. Inside is kept what is thought to be Simon's head – a gruesome relic which ought perhaps to be placed in his tomb at Canterbury. The college has disappeared except for a stone arch within a brick surround close by the tower. There are some interesting tombs in the churchyard including one by the south-east gate showing a skeleton with an hourglass and a scythe. The cottages by the south gate are the sole surviving houses from Gregory Street, the rest disappeared with the road widening in the 1960s.

The Demise of the College

For 136 years the college was efficiently run on strict lines. However, at the bishop's visitation of 1520 there were signs that all was not well. The master, John Eden, failed to make an appearance and was excommunicated. Finances appeared to be in order but discipline was lax, especially with regard to dress. In 1526 the situation had worsened. Master Richard Eden gave a good report of everything but the bishop was suspicious and adjourned the session for several weeks. Upon resuming all was in chaos. The master was not present and the annual accounts were not rendered. The steward was found to be much at fault. The brethren complained that their stipends were not paid properly and the manors and granges were not attended to.

The visitation of 1532 showed further decline and neglect and the running of the college under Master Richard Eden was nothing short of scandalous. Not surprisingly the college and its lands were surrendered to the king on the 9 December 1544.

The following year the college and all its possessions were granted to Thomas Paston, Gentleman of the Privy Chamber. He never took up residence but leased it out to George Clopton of Melford who died in 1565. Various other

people leased the buildings which had been converted and partly demolished until the Pastons sold out to John and Oliver Andrews in 1634. They leased it out to the Pannell family amongst others until it was finally sold to The Board of Guardians who converted the buildings into a workhouse for the poor of Sudbury and district. The last of the buildings were demolished in 1836 to make way for a new workhouse designed by John Brown of Norwich which subsequently became Walnuttree Hospital.

All that is left of Simon's College, a stone arch within a sixteenth-century brick surround.

The manors and granges which included Middleton Hall and Brundon Hall passed from the Paston family to the Windhams of Felbrigg in Norfolk in the mid-seventeenth century and remained with them until the 1860s.

St Peter's Church

The church stands impressively at the top of Market Hill and dominates the town. This is not surprising since the siting and the design of this building was a deliberate piece of medieval town planning conceived before the Black Death of 1348-49. It formed the centrepiece of Elizabeth de Burgh's town expansion soon after she gained control of her estate in 1322 (see p.27). The site of the church would have been pegged out before anything else and it is no accident that the main west doors open on to the great market square for this was designed as a civic church for processions and guild events. It was only after her death in 1360 that encroachments on and around the site began to detract from the original scheme. In the sixteenth century a Moot Hall would occupy the bottom half of the hill and remain for 300 years.

In the 1840s all of these encroachments were removed and Elizabeth de Burgh's original and dramatic concept recovered. The Victorians appreciated what they had found and used the open spaces to advantage. Unfortunately for us the overwhelming flow of modern traffic once again prevents us from appreciating what we have, a remarkably designed medieval town centre. On the Continent we would call it The Piazza.

It has always been said that this church was built during the years 1450-85 but we now know that this cannot be so. There were certainly at least three stages in the building and they were probably 1330-48, 1360, 1425-50. The

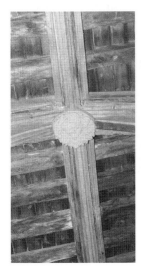

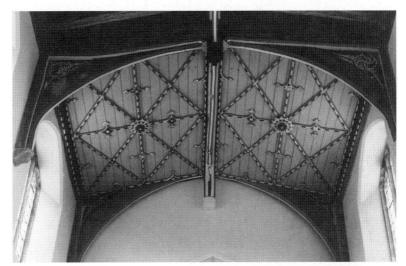

above One of three rare fourteenth-century terracotta bosses in the north aisle.

above right The eastern bay of the nave roof of St Gregory's is decorated as a canopy of honour, first for the rood but also for a nave altar.

right North aisle with chequer flint, stone flushwork and terracotta gargoyles, a unique feature for the date, *c.* 1365.

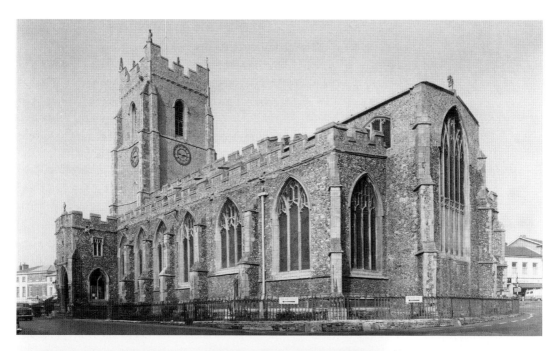

above St Peter's from the south east. A large and impressive building commenced in the mid-fourteenth century.

left The west front of St Peter's, dominating the Market Hill.

church consists of a nave and chancel, both flanked by aisles, a south porch and a west tower. Building began with the first two bays of the chancel, including the chancel arch, and the base of the tower. The tower was intended to stand beyond the west end of the nave, outside the body of the church as at All Saints and St Gregory's but with a connecting passage from north to south as at Dedham in Essex.

When this building was commenced the Decorated style was on its way out and the new Perpendicular style was coming in, simplified and with the emphasis on the vertical thrust. St Peter's is built in a curious blend of the two which helps to date it. The chancel arch is exceptionally fine with an inner moulding springing from short columns standing on brackets. This is from the Decorated period and so are the clerestory windows in the chancel but there is an additional pair from when the chancel was extended and they have the late Perpendicular depressed arch. The tracery of the windows throughout the church is highly individual and leans towards the Decorated style, but the close-set windows, the narrow buttresses, and the slender columns of the nave arcade are all early Perpendicular. Finally the massive columns which support the tower have detail on their bases identical to the fourteenth-century pillars at St Gregory's.

Exterior

The proportions are splendid and the tower is exactly the right height and size, built in three stages with angle buttresses and stepped battlements with pinnacles in the form of statues. A copper clad spire of 1810, which replaced an earlier timber spire, was removed in 1968 and there are no plans to replace it. The south porch is two storeyed and the ground floor was meant to be vaulted; the piers for the vault are still visible. The exterior stonework, including the three niches, was restored in 1911 by C.G. Hare and the three figures were inserted at the same time, they represent Christ in the act of blessing flanked by St Peter and St Gregory. The doors inside the porch as well as those on the north side are original and well carved. Several of the windows have been faithfully restored in recent years although the east window is a reconstruction from the early nineteenth century. It is blocked below the transom to allow for a classical reredos which used to be in the chancel.

Interior

If possible one should enter through the west door beneath the tower and if you are fortunate enough to find the floor clear of chairs the effect is moving and dramatic. The tower stands on three great arches so that in effect you are immediately in the nave which with the tower is six bays in length. The pillars of the nave arcade are slender with four attached shafts and moulded capitals but the detail of those on the north side differ from those opposite which indicates a time lapse in the building. Above the arcade is the five-bay clerestory but the windows are strangely out of rhythm with the arches below. The roof is very much part of the clerestory and is pitched with its five bays separated by long

arch braces supporting the tie beams. The braces spring from carved stone corbels and there is a marvellous feeling of space. The tie beams carry short king posts which support the ridge and an additional support and decorative feature is the arch bracing running along the ridge from east to west. The entire roof is ceiled and panelled with slender ribs at the intersections of which are small gilt bosses. Finally and most effectively the cornice is in the form of beautiful fan-shaped coving framing each window.

St Peter's interior looking west
A very fine building with exceptional roofs to nave and chancel.

This roof is unique in a county famous for its variety of styles but doubts were raised concerning its age from an entry in William Dowsing's diary of 1643 which states:

> St Peter's. We brake down pictures of God the Father, two crucifixes, and pictures of Christ, about one hundred in all, and gave orders to take down a cross off the steeple and diverse angels, twenty at least on the roof of the church.

It has been supposed that the last item implied that the nave roof was originally a hammer beam construction but there is no evidence to support this. Close inspection from scaffolding in 1976 revealed that the roof is basically fifteenth-century work and that if anything had been replaced in the 1685 restoration it was some of the arch bracing. It is possible that the original bracing was decorated with small angels.

This roof is the only medieval nave roof in Suffolk to be completely ceiled and panelled in its original form. Fan-shaped coving appears at Framlingham and Norwich but in both cases it disguises hammer beams; that is not the case in Sudbury.

Above the chancel arch is what purports to be a canopy of honour to the rood screen but it is not. It is formed from the cresting of the vanished screen and has been much refurbished and placed here at an uncertain date. Only part of the dado of the screen has survived but terribly repainted in the early nineteenth century. It must have been magnificent and the doorways from the loft remain and prove that it spanned the whole church from north to south.

The Aisles

The aisles are broad and form a processional route with good roofs, especially in the north aisle which has bosses and stone corbels. The principals are arch braced with carving in the spandrels. The windows are linked with a continuous stone moulding and there is a good collection of nineteenth-century stained glass. The western bays of each aisle flank the tower and were the last extensions made to the medieval church. Because of the houses which encroached on the site there are some odd angles at the western end of the north aisle.

In the south aisle is the fifteenth-century font, octagonal with each side carved with a cusped and pointed quatrefoil. During the religious upheaval of the seventeenth century it was shamefully removed and used as a horse trough but was apparently returned when the animals refused to drink from it.

The Chancel

The chancel was restored and decorated by Bodley in 1898 but his decoration of the walls was removed in 1968. It consisted mainly of the repeated motif of the crowned cross keys of St Peter on a dark red background. His reredos has survived, 20ft high and a little over 7ft in width in the Gothic style and depicting the crucifixion. It replaced the classical reredos of 1715 which consisted of a central pedimented board displaying the Ten Commandments flanked by the two paintings of Moses and Aaron by Robert Cardinall which hang over the north and south doors. Cardinall was a local artist and a pupil of Sir Godfrey Kneller.

The chancel is two bays in length with an extended sanctuary built in two periods which accounts for the astonishing inclination to the south. Between the bays are beautiful parclose screens from the fifteenth century with one light divisions which have richly carved tracery heads and carved dado. They are very similar to those in All Saints church and were once richly decorated but were repainted several times since and were finally stripped of all colour in the nineteenth century.

The ceiling of the chancel is original although recoloured by Bodley. It is flat pitched, ceiled and panelled. Along the ridge are small but detailed bosses depicting angels carrying a book, a shield and a cross. Other bosses at the inter-section of the panel ribs are in the form of faces, flowers, leaves, etc. A beau-tiful roof has been astonishingly overlooked by most of the experts including Pevsner and Munro Cautley in his magnum opus.

South Chapel

The South Chapel, sometimes called the Lady Chapel, has an unusual altar of oak and boxwood. The front is carved with the Nativity scene and the shallow reredos shows da Vinci's Last Supper. It is an early twentieth-century Flemish piece appreciated more in recent years than when it was first installed. In the south wall is a large recess which once held an image, possibly St Christopher, the patron saint of travellers. At the base of the pillar facing it is some interesting medieval graffiti including a crucifixion. It could only have been carved by persons kneeling before that image, possibly pilgrims because Sudbury was the last overnight stop on the pilgrimage route to St Edmundsbury.

Restorations

This church has been most fortunate in its restorations from which it has bene-fited enormously. We have already seen much of Bodley's work which was very sympathetic and enhanced an already beautiful church. However, we owe even more to Butterfield who was engaged by Canon Molyneux in 1858-59, a very dangerous age where restorations are concerned. Molyneux was apparently a man of taste and discrimination and was responsible for sensitive restoration work at Salter's Hall which was where he lived.

He seems to have exerted considerable control over Butterfield both here and at St Gregory's. He was also ruthless in cleansing the church of any eighteenth-century fittings and fixtures. There were formerly three wide eighteenth-century galleries, the west one under the tower which held the organ was erected at a cost of £66 15s 8d in 1777. Molyneux had all three removed and on the night of 30 March 1859 he had all the box pews taken out and sold on the Market Hill next morning. They were replaced by simple rush-seated ladder-back chairs designed by Butterfield. It was intended that just sufficient chairs were put out for each service and returned to store after use leaving the church uncluttered as it would have been in medieval days. It was a revolutionary idea conceived to show off the building to advantage.

The chancel floor was relaid and a new pulpit installed, both remarkably restrained. However, the crowning achievement was the reintroduction of stained glass to the windows. Now Victorian stained glass can be beautiful or hideous, tactful or over sentimental, beautifully toned or garish. The three windows from the Butterfield restoration are perfect and are the work of Hardman, but the relationship between the two men was not always harmonious.

When the first window was produced, the chancel east, Butterfield criticised it for lacking 'strength and force'. Hardman, not pleased with such criticism, inserted the second window under the tower without waiting for Butterfield's approval of the cartoons. Butterfield was of course furious but nevertheless commissioned a third window, the east window of the south chapel.

Towards the end of the century Hardman would be commissioned to produce more windows but the earlier ones for Butterfield are superior.

There was another major restoration in 1968 when the tower had to be rebuilt from the belfry level. The greater part of the cost was met by a legacy from Mr C.W. Worters, an ex-butcher from North Street in Sudbury. It was a splendid gift in the true spirit of the cloth merchants who first built the church. There were of course many other contributors and we have every reason to be thankful to them. There was a real danger that the tower may have been demolished and incredible though it may seem at least one person advocated that the roofs be removed and the church be allowed to become a ruin.

St Peter's was declared redundant in 1972 and after standing unused for four years was invested in the Redundant Churches Fund. It now has a new life as a cultural and social hall though still remaining a consecrated building. The Friends of St Peter's, a local charitable trust, has done much to raise funds for internal maintenance and improvements.

All Saints Church

This splendid building stands on the site of the Norman church built to serve the new parish created when the bridge was built. In 1150 it was purchased with the chapel of Ballingdon and the lands of Middleton Hall by Adam the Monk for the abbey at St Albans. It was rebuilt in the early 1300s and evidence from wills and structural remains show that it had a chancel, nave, north chancel, chapel and north aisle.

All that remains from that church are the chancel and part of the chancel chapel now used as vestries. The rest is a rebuild from the fifteenth century and the cost was met from donations given by the cloth merchants, the local gentry, and many more humble people. The will of Thomas Shorthose, a Sudbury weaver, is dated 1459 and gives the approximate date of the north aisle and also tells us that the south aisle was already built:

'...also I will when the parishioners of the aforesaid church of All Saints shall have built anew the old aisle in the north part of the same church then my executors shall pay out of my goods twenty marks for a low bench in the same north aisle so to be built anew, to be made according to the benches in the south part of the same church now existing. Also I bequeath to the fabric of the same north aisle 40 shillings...'

Joan Dennys, a widow of Sudbury, in her will dated 6 June 1460, bequeathed twenty shillings to make, 'one arch between the church and chapel on the north part of the same church'. This is the arch that still divides the north aisle from the north chapel. The last part of the church to be built was the Felton chantry chapel on the south side of the chancel which dates from about 1480.

A typical parish church in a medieval cloth town it exudes wealth and refinement from that age. It was a fashionable church in pre-Reformation times but the tombs of the many local worthies who were buried within its walls have all disappeared. It became the most fashionable church in the town again throughout the seventeenth and eighteenth centuries as the ledger slabs which pave the nave testify. There are many who have no memorial, fourteen members of the Eden family from Ballingdon Hall are buried under the organ in the north chapel. Fourteen Burkitts, whose house still stands on the corner of the lane named after them, lie under the sanctuary. Feltons, Gibbons and Fenns are resting under the chancel and the south chapel, and the Sudbury Waldegraves rest in the aisles. Sudbury's Valhalla, yet not a single tomb of distinction has survived.

Exterior

The tower is the town's finest. Built in three stages with huge angle buttresses, stepped battlements, and pinnacles in the form of seated angels. A massive stair turret at the south-east rises above the battlements and has a deep parapet. There are four large belfry windows with good perpendicular tracery, a west window to light the nave and especially fine carved west doors. There is a fine octave of bells with few rivals with regard to tone.

The south aisle was built in two stages and it is not difficult to see where they meet. The first four windows nearest the tower form the aisle and they date from around 1440 and the next two belong to the Felton chantry of around 1480. All the windows have identical, excellent and refined perpendicular tracery and there are hood moulds with carved stone heads as stops. Note the hooded monk, the knight in chain mail, and the smiling lady.

The seventeenth-century brick porch was demolished in the nineteenth century because it was considered 'unworthy'. Before recent restoration the battlements displayed much worn arms of donors. On the north side some of the windows have been carefully restored (1978-79). The doors are excellent with carved tracery panels and a trailing vine surround. At the north-east corner is the two-storeyed vestry built within the remains of what was a fourteenth-century chapel. High up in the east wall can be seen the outline of an arched window with a smaller window inserted.

Interior

Impressive and yet homely, the pillars rising above a sea of nineteenth-century pews with carved poppy heads. A beautifully proportioned arcade of five bays with slender pillars identical to those at St Peter's – four attached shafts with finely moulded capitals. Here the arch mouldings are late perpendicular and they are decorated with shields, fleurons and crowns. Above them is the clerestory of five bays crowned with an excellent cambered tie-beam roof. All the principal rafters are moulded but alternate ones are arch-braced, those not braced once terminated with angels, which makes one wonder whether Dowsing made a mistake in his diary with regard to St Peter's. He doesn't mention the roof here, but the angels have gone and only a little of the cresting

An unusual painted pedigree of the Eden family of Ballingdon Hall and The Priory, at All Saints. Until the nineteenth century it had a marble surround.

remains. Binoculars, a must for close inspection, will reveal the whole roof has traces of colour and decoration. There are spiral bands, stars, arrows on the rafters pointing to the ridge and traces of an inscription along the wall plate which has been erased.

High up by the chancel arch is the blocked doorway which shows the position of the loft above the rood screen. Both loft and screen have gone but panels have survived and are incorporated in the modern tower screen. Others were re-used for the reading desks. The pulpit dates from 1450 and is in a remarkably good state of preservation because it was boxed in when the church was filled with high-backed box pews in the seventeenth century. It was rediscovered and restored in 1840. It is octagonal with tracery panels and slender buttresses and there is a rich battlemented cornice and elegant trumpet shaped stem. The sacred monogram is modern as is the staircase. Pulpits of this date are not common and rarely are they so well preserved.

The font is a good example of the traditional East Anglian type with tracery panels to bowl and shaft. Its cupboard type painted cover, similar to those at Boxford and Bramford, was destroyed in the nineteenth century. The angel lectern of carved oak is a memorial to those of the parish who gave their lives in the First World War.

North Aisle

There are two outstanding features, the roof and the parclose screen. The roof, like that in the nave, is a cambered tie beam construction. All the principal rafters rest on carved corbels representing birds, angels, human heads, etc. and alternate principals are arch braced. There are splendid carved bosses and every rafter is moulded. There is a battlemented cornice with delicate fleur-de-lis cresting. This is a very high quality roof of the period.

One of four beautiful carved
screens in All Saints, c. 1450.

The superb screen separates the aisle from the chapel and stands beneath the
arch paid for by Joan Dennys in 1460. A centre broad arch with cusping is
flanked by two narrower openings on either side, all with rich open tracery heads
and much carved foliage and very slender buttress shafts and a top rail with
trailing vine and fleur-de-lis cresting. The dado has eleven divisions, seven with
carved tracery but the four nearest the wall remain blank because an altar stood
in front of it there. The screen would have been highly coloured when it was new
and so was the eastern bay of the roof above it where traces can be seen.

The large tomb slab in front of the screen with the indent for a brass showing
a man and his two wives marks the grave of Sir Edward Waldegrave. Charles
Badham, a nineteenth-century vicar, had the name of Thomas Eden cut into the
stone in error. It is high time this was put to rights.

South Aisle

This aisle is narrower than the north aisle and earlier with a good roof, similar to
the nave but with carved corbels to all principals and no bosses. The screen is a
narrower version of that seen in the north aisle with only one light either side of
the broad centre arch. Similar tracery heads and top rail with cresting. Dado with
tracery panels on the north side only, those on the south side are plain and a
piscina set into the wall confirms the site of an altar here.

John Waldegrave was buried in front of this screen in 1543. Part of his tomb,
destroyed in the seventeenth century, can be seen just above the wainscoting
nearby.

South Chapel

This was built as a chantry chapel for John Felton and has been much abused
in the past. There is an inappropriate wood block floor under the carpet which

ought to be removed. Underneath it are the black marble ledger slabs of the Gibbon family who took over this chapel in the eighteenth century. They blocked the east window here to accommodate a wall monument to John Gibbon (d.1744) suitably inscribed with details of his charitable work. It is bedecked with swags, scrolls, and cherubs and is now housed beneath the tower. The chapel was then used to house the organ until 1882 when a new east window was inserted and the present floor laid. John Felton's tomb slab lies by the wall against the screen.

There is a good piscina by the priest's door and the arch into the chancel was created about 1480. The roof here is plain but was originally ceiled and painted. Another richly carved parclose screen fills the arch into the chancel.

The Chancel

The chancel was built in around 1300 in the Decorated style of that period and consequently probably the oldest building in Sudbury. It has two original arches on the north side with polygonal pillars and moulded capitals. One arch has been blocked to allow the north chapel to be rebuilt as vestries. The clerestory windows were blocked when the chapels were rebuilt. There is a good plain roof which was raised 2ft in 1882 when the large east window was inserted. All the furnishings date from 1882 but the holy table in the sanctuary is a fine Jacobean example. The fine parclose screen against the organ has been resited and extended to include a doorway in the nineteenth century.

On the south wall is a pedimented wall monument to the Fenn family (1818) of Ballingdon. Beneath it is a plaque depicting the parable of the Good Samaritan. The plaque is by John Bacon jnr and the monument is signed by Manning.

At this altar in November 1748 Frances Carter, daughter of William Carter of Ballingdon, married Robert Andrews, the young squire at Auberies on Ballingdon Hill. They were made immortal by Thomas Gainsborough who painted their wedding portrait against the backdrop of Sudbury and the Stour valley. The picture hangs in the National Gallery in London. A fortnight after the wedding her father died and was buried at Bulmer.

North Chapel

Although almost impossible to study because it houses the organ it is nevertheless a very interesting chapel. It is now half its original size because the eastern half has been converted into two chambers, one above the other. The conversion took place when the Felton chantry was built in around 1480. Before then it had been divided horizontally in the form of a loft with screens and the upper level was lit by a large window, the outline of which can be seen outside. The blocked arch in the sanctuary has its pillars encased in order to support the loft and the screen which overlooked the sanctuary is resited lower down against the organ. A similar arrangement exists at Wingfield in east Suffolk.

The chapel originally belonged to the Waldegrave family but through marriage became the burial chapel of the Edens of Ballingdon Hall and The Priory.

1 above The Chantry and Salter's Hall range in Stour Street, all of which are from around 1450 except for the centre gable which is from around 1380.

2 right A carved corner post at The Chantry which supports the dragon beam inside.

3 *opposite above* The fourteenth-century Salter's Hall. Beneath the gable on the right was originally a wagon entrance.

4 *opposite below* Salter's Hall, built in around 1450, is one of the finest houses of its period in the country.

5 *above left* Fifteenth-century carved window tracery at Salter's Hall.

6 *above right* The beautiful oriel window with carved soffit and original tracery of 1450.

7 *below* Fifteenth-century cottages in Stour Street, facing the site of the Saxon market.

8 opposite above Fifteenth-century cottages in Stour Street. The end house has lost its great hall to make way for Victorian almshouses which have since been demolished to make a car park.

9 opposite below Stour Hall in Stour Street, now called Cleeve Hall, but originally built in around 1450 on the site of the early medieval manor house when this street was called Stourhallstreet.

10 above The old tannery, once the home of the Sparrow family and built on the edge of the Great Ditch where it joined the river at Mill Hill.

11 above The nineteenth-century grammar school, now William Wood House, in Christopher Lane.

12 opposite above Seventeenth-century Flemish-style houses with stuccoed walls in Friar's Street. The brick house next door stands on the site of the eighteenth-century gaol.

13 opposite below Ballingdon Hall (*c.* 1590) on its new site. The first floor was the long gallery which led off the great chamber, represented by the right-hand bay.

14 opposite above The house of Mr Bullock who gave land to the Quakers for their Meeting House. Until it was built they met in an upper room here. The bow window and the fanlight over the door are of eighteenth-century cast iron.

15 opposite below Abraham Griggs, a cloth merchant, married Susannah Gainsborough, the painter's aunt, and moved into this house in Cross Street in 1689. The adjoining houses were part of his warehouse. It remained in the family until the nineteenth century and bunting from this building was used to make Stars and Stripes which flew over Fort Lauderdale.

16 above left Pretty Georgian bay windows in Friar's Street on much older houses.

17 above right Medieval roofs at the rear of the same houses in Friar's Street betray their origins.

18 below Buzzard's Hall in Friar's Street was originally the Wool Hall in the fifteenth century. It was remodelled in the sixteenth century and later became the home of Thomas Gainsborough, uncle to his namesake the painter.

19 opposite above A fine Geogian shopfront in Balingdon Street, one of several which have survived in this street.

20 opposite below Fourteenth-century cottages in Middleton Road, Ballingdon – possibly the oldest in the town.

21 above St Gregory's tower which contains recently identified Saxon bricks from the earlier church. They can clearly be seen in the bottom left corner of this picture.

22 left St Gregory's font cover, telescoped for access to the font.

23 below St Gregory's angel from the chancel ceiling, showing the instruments of The Passion, here the ladder

24 The old Rising Sun in Plough Lane. This is a heavily disguised medieval hall house clothed in nineteenth-century red brick. Plough Lane was opened up to give access into the New Quarter when the first Ballingdon bridge was built in the twelfth century.

25 The memorial in honour of those who served and the 400 men who died from the 486th Bombardment Group (H) based at Chilton in 1944/5. Dedicated 4 July 1987 it is situated beside the war memorial outside the gate of St Gregory's.

26 The nave of St Peter's church being used to house a history exhibition in 2001.

27 *above* The Old Moot Hall in Cross Street, used for town meetings by the mayor and aldermen until replaced by a new Moot Hall on Market Hill in Mary Tudor's reign. It was probably still used for civic purposes in the reign of James I.

28 *right* The original doorway to the stone-flagged passage. The house was restored after the Second World War and is now a well-cared for private house.

29 *overleaf* Side view of The Old Moot Hall. The upper floor was the great meeting room.

THE
OLD
MOOT
HALL

On the east wall is painted the family tree of the Edens showing their connections with the Waldegrave, St Clere, Peyton and other local families through various coats of arms. At one time it was framed by marble pillars standing on a ledge and bearing a rich entablature. It was enclosed within an iron palisade with a gate to the north. A splendid piece of seventeenth-century vanity, it was begun in 1615 and completed two years later. Charles Badham claimed that it was in a dilapidated state and had it removed in about 1840. He erected a black marble slab nearby inscribed with the names of the Edens who were buried in the chapel.

Sadly the wall painting is suffering damage and needs urgent attention to prevent further deterioration. Many of the colours have changed because of the lime in the plaster but it appears to be a unique survival. The roof of the chapel is excellent and is more or less a continuation of the north aisle. The vestry door is fifteenth century work.

The Churchyard

The churchyard is a quiet oasis in this part of town. The last burial was in 1857 and considering the number interred over the years comparatively few tombstones have survived. On the north side a massive box tomb dominates with baluster corners, obviously eighteenth century, it marks the vault wherein are buried eleven members of the Gainsborough family, including their Hassell and Fenn relatives beginning with William Hassell in 1708 to Mary Gainsborough in 1769.

On the opposite side of the path and fronting the vicarage there is but one memorial. It would be nice to see another commemorating the deaths of eighty-four parishioners who died of smallpox in the epidemic of 1737 and are buried here.

The vicarage is mainly a seventeenth-century building within an eighteenth-century brick casing but the porch is Victorian. In the entrance hall some panelling from the Waldegrave house, which stood on the site of the parish hall, has been assembled to form a dado. It dates from the late sixteenth and early seventeenth century and includes two profile busts of a man and a woman and who are believed to be Dutch or Flemish. There is also an excellent seventeenth-century staircase which rises in one flight and branches off into two return flights, it is in situ and did not come from the Waldegrave house as is often claimed.

Summary

It is clear that for the first three quarters of the fifteenth century there was a great deal of building activity going on in Sudbury, much of it with regard to the churches. In the last decade the craftsmen would turn to Melford, just three miles away, where the building of the great and magnificent church of The Holy Trinity had begun. Three miles further on work was in progress on the new church at Lavenham, also magnificent, and there would be a continual friendly

rivalry between the two. The three churches of Sudbury, treasure houses when in their prime, would be overshadowed by the sheer scale and unique character of those buildings. They still are, but it is rather like comparing a Constable painting with a da Vinci.

All Saints, south side, a fifteenth-century re-build with typical East Anglian Perpendicular tracery to the windows.

One should also remember that apart from the three churches Sudbury had a Benedictine priory, a Dominican friary, a hospital, a college for priests, and Holy Sepulchre chapel.

The Dominican priory church was of considerable size and it had a belfry tower. All of these were swept away in the next century as the Reformation exploded over Europe. There would be new learning and Sudbury acquired a Grammar School thanks to William Wood.

Chantry Chapels in Sudbury

Chantry chapels were founded and endowed with money, land, and other possessions so that masses and prayers might be sung for the founder and his family. They usually take the form of a side chapel built alongside the chancel, as was the Felton chantry in All Saints. Sometimes they are a screened off section of an aisle with an altar and far less commonly they are an independent building not attached to any church. Whatever the case they were usually very well endowed to ensure their maintenance and to adequately compensate the chantry priest or chaplain who was to say the mass and prayers. Some of them were also established to include the founding of grammar schools.

John Felton's chantry was endowed with lands in Ballingdon, Bulmer, Henny, Borley and Liston worth eight pounds ten shillings per annum in 1520. It has been estimated that about 2,000 such chapels were founded between the thirteenth century and the Reformation. Collectively they represented a considerable pool of assets and Henry VIII was on the point of taking them over when he died. It was his son Edward VI who finally appropriated them in 1548 and redistributed some of the income to found and endow grammar schools all over the country bearing his name.

It does seem possible that the Chapel of The Holy Sepulchre (see p.18) may have been founded as a chantry. It was certainly endowed with land and it had its own chaplain. In the Ecclesiastical Survey of 1534 its annual value was given as forty shillings. In 1551 Edward VI gave the chapel, messuage and land of St Sepulchre to his friend and tutor Sir John Cheke and that is the last we hear of it. If it was a chantry then it was intended to perpetuate prayers for the souls of the Gloucester dynasty.

Sudbury Grammar School

William Wood, master of the college, died in 1491 and his will was proved on 28 July 1493. In it he made provision for the school's foundation and appointed four feoffees to carry out his instructions.

They were given a dwelling house with croftlands 'formerly belonging to John Hilles situated along a lane leading from the Preaching Friars as far as the church of St Gregory (School Street). Between the tenements of John Roberts Senior, the tenement of Robert Maldon, the tenement of John Chapman on the north side and the lane called Wylewerlelane (Christopher Lane) on the south side...'.

The feoffees were to co-opt sixteen other persons nominated by the warden of the college. Their task was to see that the master of the college should 'hire and nominate an honest and honourable man to dwell in the said messuage and teach Grammar and the same continuously and daily to educate boys and others able to profit at the school for ever'.

The Master of Grammar was to receive the yearly outgoings and profits of the messuage and garden, but was to pay ten shillings a year to the warden of the college to be used for the repair and maintenance of the property. Latin and grammar were the main subjects taught but to these were added rhetoric, Greek and religious instruction. All under the watchful eye of the college master.

When the college was closed the new owners became Patrons of the Living and as such took on the responsibilities due to the school. Thus began the long tradition of curates from St Gregory's acting as schoolmaster at the grammar school. Probably the best known was Thomas Gainsborough's uncle, Humphrey Burrough, who was master when his nephew was a scholar.

At some time the school had acquired a farm at Maplestead about which a dispute arose causing the school to close in 1841. The patron, Sir Lachlan Maclean insisted that the farm belonged to him and not the school. A lawsuit starting in 1830 and ending in 1856 decided in favour of the school. The dispute being settled the old timber-framed schoolhouse was pulled down and new buildings designed by a Mr Pope were erected. The builder was Charles Fordham of Melford and the cost was £2,300. At this time the long tradition of curate masters was also brought to an end. The school reopened in 1858 and was placed under a governing body in the late 1870s and was eventually transferred to the county council in 1909. New buildings were erected in 1941 and more temporary buildings were supplied in the 1960s. In 1972 the school finally closed and the pupils transferred to the new upper school. The buildings were demolished except for Pope's building which has been adapted and new buildings erected to form secure sheltered housing for the elderly as William Wood House.

The Sudbury Embroideries

These priceless treasures belong to St Gregory's church but at the time of writing are in the care of Ipswich Museum. For about twenty years they were displayed in St Peter's but were removed to the protection of the museum when the church was declared redundant. Of the two pieces the most important is The Sudbury Pall, a ceremonial cloth of embroidered velvet which was placed over a coffin during the burial service of important persons. It dates from the latter

The rare and beautiful Sudbury embroideries are stored away in Ipswich Museum until suitable arrangements can be made for their display. Here they are shown as they used to be seen in St Peter's church.

half of the fifteenth century and is an especially fine example of English church embroidery from that period.

Strangely the very first mention we have of the cloth appears in the old Town Book of 18 December 1569 where it states: 'John Rushbrooke of Borehamgate gave up two spouts of lead weighing 135lbs and a cloth of gold and velvet called The Pall which did belong to the church of St Peter aforesaid, being taken from there by the said John Rushbrooke to recover payment for certain charges he had been at for the said church, which he now agreed to remit.'

It next appears in an inventory for St Peter's in 1675 described as 'one burying cloth embroidered with gold and silver'. Only in the late eighteenth century do we see it described as 'The Aldermen's Pall' on a label attached to it which states 'The Aldermen's Pall repaired 1784'.

The unique ceiled and painted roof in the nave at St Peter's.

It is interesting to note that the first description places the emphasis on gold. This can be explained for close scrutiny of the flat surface shows clear evidence that a large area was covered originally with an embroidered crucifixion. This would have been worked in gold thread but crucifixions shown in any form were banned in the mid-seventeenth century so it would have been carefully unpicked and the valuable gold thread salvaged. The second description of 1675 is more appropriate for the pall as seen today.

The pall is made from maroon silk velvet which would have been imported from Italy. The side and end folds are embroidered with elegant stylised vases of lilies in gold and silver thread. Each fold also has a kneeling figure in a shroud worked in coloured silks. Each figure has a prayer scroll encircling its head. The prayers are quotations from the Vulgate, the Latin Bible. Translated into modern English they read as follows:

St Peter's porch restored in 1911 by C.G. Hare.

'I Trust in thy Light to lighten my darkness'
'Heal thou my Soul O Lord for I have sinned against Thee'
'Though I have sinned I hope to see the Goodness of The Lord'
'Haste Thee to help me O Lord'

These are supplications from the dead person direct to his Saviour. Had they been requests for others to pray for their souls then the pall would not have survived the seventeenth century.

The pall is edged with a fringe of coloured silks which was probably added in the eighteenth century and may well be the 'repair' mentioned above.

Throughout the early Middle Ages English embroidery using gold and silver thread was famous throughout Europe and called Opus Anglicanum. A Vatican inventory of 1295 lists over 100 pieces. One of the most famous embroiderers was Mabel of St Edmundsbury who regularly appears as working for Henry III in the period 1239-44. Much of this work was done by nuns in religious houses but by the fifteenth century specialised workshops were established in various parts of the kingdom employing men. The Sudbury Pall would have come from such a place.

How did St Peter's come to own such a piece? The most logical answer is that it was probably made for the college for the burial service of a master and was passed to the church after the Reformation. It may well have been commissioned by William Wood, if so it would have been used for the first time at his own burial in 1491.

The Pulpit Cloth

From the time of Henry VIII it was compulsory for churches to display the Royal Arms to acknowledge the sovereign as head of the church in England. Sometimes they were painted on board or carved in wood and many have survived.

When St Peter's was restored in 1685, the same year that James II came to the throne, a new set of arms was provided in the form of an embroidered panel on velvet. For display purposes the panel was mounted on some other panels cut from a cope which the church owned and had no further use. The whole ensemble was then suspended from the pulpit which had become the focal point of church services and not the altar as in pre-Reformation days.

The arms are beautifully worked in coloured silks and below them is a smaller version of the borough arms. The panels which were cut from the cope are of Italian silk from the late fifteenth or early sixteenth centuries. We know of two such copes in the possession of St Peter's at one time. Simon Danown, in his will dated 1457, leaves six shillings and eight pence towards payment for 'new copes bought for the church of St Peter'. Another wealthy man, Thomas Easton of Sudbury, donated an embroidered cope to the church in 1503.

Conservation work was done on these valuable pieces prior to their temporary display at a history exhibition arranged by Sudbury History Society in May 2003. This was the first time the public had the opportunity to view them for thirty years. They have been returned to the care of Ipswich Museum until a more permanent display can be arranged.

chapter five

Sixteenth century

The Reformation and Sudbury

The great religious revolution of the sixteenth century which saw the establish-ment of the Protestant churches and known as The Reformation was long overdue. It was of course precipitated in England by the desire of Henry VIII for a male heir and the subsequent desire for a divorce to help him achieve that purpose. The final break with Rome and the establishment of the monarch as the supreme head of the Church in England affected the lives of every person in the land. It seems incredible to us that no English version of the Bible existed when Henry came to the throne in 1509 and one can well imagine the shock and wonder when the first copies of Tyndale's English translation of the New Testament were smuggled into England from Antwerp and read. They had to wait until 1539 before the full translated Bible was ordered to be placed in every church. In 1543 an Act of Parliament was passed which prohibited the lower classes from reading the Bible because Henry considered unrestricted reading of the scriptures dangerous, which of course it was.

People's lives had been strictly controlled by the Church but now the simple Christian message was suddenly accessible and the whole of the Papal dogma was exposed to scrutiny. In modern parlance the ordinary man in the street was gradually realising that for centuries he had been deceived. There are countless books dealing with all aspects of The Reformation and there is only space here to observe some of the consequences which affected the town of Sudbury. Top of the list must surely be the suppression of the religious houses in 1539 which saw the end of the Dominican priory and the demolition of its church in Friar's Street. Just three years before the Benedictine priory of St Bartholomew had been closed down and rented out by Westminster. In 1544 The college was surrendered to the Crown with all its lands.

Even the closure of the great abbey at St Edmundsbury, which owned vast tracts of West Suffolk, including the neighbouring village of Long Melford where the abbott had his country seat, was to have an impact. Right up to the end the shrine of St Edmund had attracted a steady stream of pilgrims and Sudbury was the last overnight stopping place en route. It had several inns which depended on that trade to a great extent. Much of the land surrounding Sudbury was now in the hands of strangers, Middleton and Brundon, no longer the property of the college, belonged to absentee landlords the Paston family in Norfolk. A lawyer and clerk to the Star Chamber, Sir Thomas Eden, was given the priory where he promptly moved into the prior's house and purchased Ballingdon Hall from the Pastons. The priory of St Bartholomew was given back to the re-named collegiate church of St Peter at Westminster as part of their endowment.

Lawyers did rather well out of the redistribution of church lands, William Cordell, a lawyer in the employment of Henry VIII, managed to rent the manor of Melford where the abbot had built a magnificent hall, later he would become Master of the Rolls and be given the manor outright for his services to Henry VIII, Edward VI, and Mary.

Edward Waldegrave and Sudbury's Royal Charter from Queen Mary

Cordell was a clever man, he managed to serve four of the Tudor monarchs and still die in his bed a rich and respected man. Others were not so fortunate. Cardinal Wolsey from Ipswich became the most powerful man in the land after the king, but died in disgrace. In Sudbury there was a house in Church Street, where All Saints parish hall now stands, which was the home of a branch of the Waldegrave family from Smallbridge Hall in Bures. Here was born Edward Waldegrave, the son of John Waldegrave, in 1520. Through influential relatives he found a place at court and eventually became a principal officer in the household of the Princess Mary.

When Henry VIII died and was succeeded by his son Edward VI, England became a Protestant nation and Mary, because she would not renounce her faith and remained a staunch Catholic, was in grave danger. At that time she was living at Copt Hall in Essex and it was no secret that she and her household were attending Mass in her private chapel. Edward Waldegrave, with Sir Robert Rochester his uncle, and Sir Robert Englefield were commanded by the king to prevent her from doing so. They were not successful and Waldegrave, being a staunch Catholic himself, would have been most reluctant to pursue the task. Because of their failure they were committed first to the Fleet prison and afterwards to the Tower.

Edward only reigned for five years and when he died Mary was living at Hunsdon House in Hertfordshire. He died on 6 July 1533 but news of his death was suppressed for four days while the Duke of Northumberland put into action his plans to place his daughter-in-law Lady Jane Grey on the throne. Mary was informed that her brother was dying when in fact he was already dead. She left Hunsdon to be at his bedside but was met at Hoddesdon by someone who told her of the trap that was set for her. She immediately turned about and made her way to Kenninghall in Norfolk, stopping en route at Sawston Hall owned by the

Catholic Huddlestons. Eventually she moved on to Framlingham Castle where she raised her standard and had herself proclaimed Queen. Northumberland was not popular and most of the country was in favour of Mary and that included Sudbury.

Edward Waldegrave raised a considerable contingent from Sudbury and joined Mary at Framlingham and then escorted her into London to claim her throne. For this act Sudbury was granted a charter dated 30 May 1554 recognizing and confirming to the borough all the rights and privileges of a corporate town. From this charter we learn:

> Our town of Sudbury is an old and ancient town, having in it from time out of mind for the better ruling and government of the same one mayor, six aldermen, four and twenty burgesses, two sergeants, one bailiff, two constables, and other common officers, by which the men and inhabitants thereof from time out of mind have been ruled and governed.

Sir Edward Waldegrave's progress at court saw him made a privy councillor, Master of the Wardrobe, and eventually Chancellor of the Dutchy of Lancaster. He was already in possession of the manor of Borley but to this was added Navestock in Essex, Chewton in Somerset, Hever Castle in Kent and various other commissions and posts. However, Mary's reign lasted but five years and with the accession of Elizabeth, who was a Protestant, he was deprived of all his honours and he retired to Borley. Two years later he was arrested and taken with his wife to the Tower on a charge of celebrating Mass in their house at Borley but he was not well and died there on the third of September. He was buried within the Tower and Lady Waldegrave was released. Later she had his body removed to Borley where it lies in a sumptuous tomb.

The Moot Hall and Market Place

Shortly after acquiring their charter from Mary the mayor and corporation celebrated by erecting a handsome timber-framed Moot Hall which was a serious encroachment on the foot of the Market Hill. Next to it was the Corn Market and then the houses which now encircled the church so that the great open square of Elizabeth de Burgh was lost for 300 years.

The market was reduced to the areas north and east of the church. What is now Old Market Place in front of the town hall was the butter market, while the leather sellers and shoemakers had their stalls and shops abutting the church. The butchers' shambles was to the south-east of the church in the centre of what is now King Street. Below there was an open brook known as The Gull and the butchers were often fined for throwing offal and waste material into it. The brook is still there but in the form of an underground flood drain which disgorges at Friar's Meadow.

Surrounding the market were the inns and taverns which formed such an important part of the town's life. To the south of the church was the Crown Inn,

A view of Market Hill before the clearance that followed the Town Improvement Act of 1826.

later to be re-named The Rose and Crown, built three sides round a great courtyard and frequently used for mayoral banquets. Facing the butter market was the George and Dragon, later renamed The George Inn after the first of the Hanoverians. The Chequers Inn occupied the site of the present town hall.

At the foot of the hill was the great White Hart with frontages on Sepulchre Street (now Gainsborough Street) and Market Hill. Rowland Taylor, the Rector of Hadleigh, spent one night under its roof shortly before being burned at the stake on Aldham Common in Mary's reign. A few yards beyond it in Sepulchre Street and on the corner of Christopher Lane was The Angel Inn with the Christopher Tavern on the opposite corner of the lane. Around the corner in Friar's Street, next door to the White Hart, was The Anchor. Many more would be added to this list in the eighteenth century.

The new Moot Hall is only known to us through watercolours and drawings of the early nineteenth century. They show a double-gabled structure facing St Peter's church of which the left hand portion appears to be an independent shop though it may have been part of the Moot Hall originally. The gable of the second portion was covered with a huge rendition of the Royal Arms. Beneath is an oriel window of twelve lights filling the full width of the façade. On the ground floor is the main door and a broad timber arch which indicates that it may at one time have been used as a covered market. By the nineteenth century it had been closed in and a run of lock-up shops filled the space. A charming bell cupola crowned the gable.

Sudbury. Corn Exchange (Market Day)

Market day in front of the Corn Exchange in 1904 – no traffic but plenty of people.

The council chamber filled the first floor which also acted as a courtroom. At the far end, facing the window, was a raised dais to accommodate a table and chairs for the mayor and aldermen. For the first fifty years the hall was also used for the performance of plays but received much damage as a result. It was thoroughly restored in 1607 and thereafter the performance of plays in the Moot Hall was banned and they moved into the inn yards.

A new town hall was built in 1828 and two years later the Moot Hall was sold to the Paving and Lighting Commissioners for £300 so that it could be demolished and the site cleared.

In the Town Books stored at the Record Office at St Edmundsbury are recorded many payments to visiting actors or players between the years 1574-1622. The Earl of Sussex, Lord Sheffield, Lord Oxenford, The Earls of Leicester, all had players performing here at some time. Likewise The King's Players, The Queen's Players, The Prince's Players and The Children of the Revells are all recorded. In 1658 the hall was treated to a new green carpet and thirty-two new green cushions from the mayor and corporation.

The Town Books are a fascinating record of the general running of the town, the strict control of the traders, weights and measures, town cleanliness or the lack of it, paying for the Grant of Arms from Elizabeth, trips to London to check records at the Tower. They commenced in Elizabeth's reign and go through to the nineteenth century but there are serious gaps.

Ballingdon Hall, a Great Elizabethan House

Sometime around 1590 Sir Thomas Eden of The Priory set about rebuilding Ballingdon Hall on a very grand scale. It was to be completed by 1593 ready to be occupied by his newly wedded son Thomas and his bride Mary Darcy of Tiptree Priory. The plan was based on the letter H with a central hall block and far projecting wings to back and front. A remarkable fact is that the building was for the most part timber-framed although all the other great mansions in the area were being constructed with fashionable red brick.

Sperling was incorrect when he described the surviving portion as the 'central crossing of the H'. The house faced east towards Middleton and what has survived is the northern cross-wing. This explains the complete absence of a major entrance doorway or porch. The impressive façade of the house we see today was originally a side elevation, the central hall block and a matching wing to the south were demolished after a fire in 1741, when the remaining parts became a farmhouse.

The house became internationally famous in 1972 when it was raised on a steel platform and winched to a new site 200 yards further up Ballingdon Hill and away from the encroaching industrial and housing development which threatened to surround it. In preparation for the move the chimney stacks were demolished and the decorative brick plinths beneath the bay windows carefully dismantled and stored. The internal brick walls of the eighteenth century were also taken down so what remained to be moved was the original timber-framed structure and the true nature of the building was revealed.

Ballingdon Hall on its original site, *c.* 1914.

The rear of Ballingdon Hall photographed in the 1960s. The large chimney on the right shows evidence of a lost brick façade to the vanished central hall block.

The façade should be studied first of all. It is magnificent with four canted bays soaring up to the roof with brick plinths, each of a different design. Three of the bays are capped with barge-boarded gables and carved bressummers, the fourth reaches the eaves but has no gable. There are typical carved scroll brackets and beneath the eaves is a continuous band of windows which gives the impressions that the roof is floating on glass. Many of these were blocked up to avoid the window tax imposed in the eighteenth century but they are all exposed now. There are large areas of glass forming the bay windows on both floors and more windows set in the gables, an extraordinary and extravagant display of windows for the side elevation of a house. The positioning of the chimneys before the move was a pointer but not understood. They were ranged along the back of the house, none of them penetrating the roof as they do now.

An astonishing revelation was that the first floor of this surviving wing was the Long Gallery and Great Chamber of the mansion. This explains the great glazed bays looking over the Stour Valley towards Sudbury and the reason why the chimneys were so positioned along the opposite wall, thus creating a very necessary and fashionable feature for a mansion of that period and it must be one of the last timber-framed galleries to have been built. The main room on the ground floor, judging by the screen and balustrade above it, was probably a dining room leading to a withdrawing room and library.

Obviously it was not possible for the gallery to be restored to its original function, it would have left the house with no bedrooms, but the gallery effect has been maintained partially by a corridor. The house has otherwise been restored beautifully with new slight additions blending so well it is difficult to distinguish between the old and the new. Before the move there was clear evidence that the missing hall wing did in fact have a brick façade.

The Edens of Ballingdon Hall

C.F.D. Sperling's notes to Essex Arch. Soc., 1926.

Sir Thomas Eden, for whom the Hall was built, was MP for Sudbury in 1603 and knighted for his services a year later. He died in January 1616 leaving a family of twelve young children to be brought up by their mother Mary, Lady Eden. She was a very religious woman described by a contemporary as 'a devout woman who much frequented lectures' as the sermons of the day were called. Her son John Eden grew up to be a supporter of the Parliamentary Party in the Civil War. He married, at the age of twenty-two, Ann Harlakenden of Colne Priory and in 1643 was chosen to be one of the Parliamentary Committee of the county.

It was while attending a meeting of the committee at Chelmsford on 2 June 1648 that he and eight others were captured by the Royalists and carried as hostages to Colchester, where they endured the dangers and much of the privations of the siege until released on 27 August following. It was due to him that Puritan preachers were installed in the vicarage of All Saints of which he was the patron.

One John Wilson, a Puritan lecturer in Sudbury, with a party of Sudbury men, sailed in March 1630 for New England. A number of them are recorded to have died owing to the sickness and privation on the voyage, among them 'Jeff. Ruggles and divers others of that town'.

The name of John Eden may be seen in most of the parish registers of this neighbourhood, as far off even as Castle Hedingham and Halstead, as the magistrate before whom many of the civil marriages took place. The parties to be married appear to have come to Ballingdon Hall for the ceremony although entries of the marriage were made in the registers of their respective parishes. For instance, in the Bulmer register:

> Thos. Brand of Bulmer and Penelope Everidd were married at Ballingdon Hall in the County of Essex by John Eden Esq. one of the Justices of the Peace for ye said County Ao 1656 April 29 Jo Eden.

The following entries of a later date, from the parish register of Great Maplestead, of marriages which took place at Ballingdon Hall in 1718, are difficult to explain:

> Benjamin Rownalls of this parish widower and Hannah Crabb of the parish of Hedingham Sibyll Spinster were married January 2nd 1718 at Ballingdon Hall by Mr Robert Kingsbury without license or certificate of the publication of ye banns of marriage.
>
> Item: Joseph Beak of this Parish Bachelor and Elizabeth Brand of the same Spinster were married by the same Mr Robert Kingsbury at Ballingdon Hall without either license or a certificate of ye Banns of Marriage Feb. twentieth 1718.

John Eden died at the age of seventy-five in 1683, but all his children predeceased him. His daughter Anne, wife of Jeffrey Littel of Halstead, alone left issue

so her eldest son John Littel succeeded his grandfather at Ballingdon Hall. The Littels continued to live here until 1741, when George Sawbridge Littel, who had succeeded to the property, having met with financial difficulties, the estate was sold to an ancestor of the present owner (Sperling of Dynes Hall, Great Maplestead). The house appears to have been allowed to fall into a bad state of repair, so that it became necessary to pull a great part of it down to adapt it as a farmhouse.

The Destruction of the Bridge

The all-important Ballingdon Bridge, built by the Gloucesters, survived until 1549 when it is recorded in the Town Book on 4 September:

> Ballingdon Bridge was broken up by a sudden inundation and now remains in a ruinous condition, so that people cannot cross with carts and cattle. It cannot be proved what Hundred, Parish, Body Politic or Person is responsible for the repair. For want of such knowledge the Jury say that the Town of Sudbury should repair half and the inhabitants of the County of Essex the other half.

opposite above and below Ballingdon Hall on the move to a new site further up the hill, in 1972.

below The timber bridge at Ballingdon in 1900. The river is in flood. The houses on the left are on the site of the medieval hospital. When they were later demolished some very fine carved timbers were revealed but unfortunately not kept. This bridge was replaced by a concrete structure in 1910.

The hospital nearby, which had collected tolls and had probably maintained the bridge had been closed by Henry VIII some nine years previously. The repairs were carried out using pre-used stone which may well have come from the site of the demolished priory church a few hundred yards downstream. However, the compromise reached by the jury was to create problems for the next 300 years, Sudbury and Essex rarely agreeing on matters relating to the maintenance of the structure.

From the Town Books:

> October 9 1598: One Hundred Pounds to be borrowed and laid out in making and finishing half the Bridge called Ballingdon Bridge.
> October 5 1615: The Bridge, commonly called Sudbury Great Bridge over The Stower is ruinous.

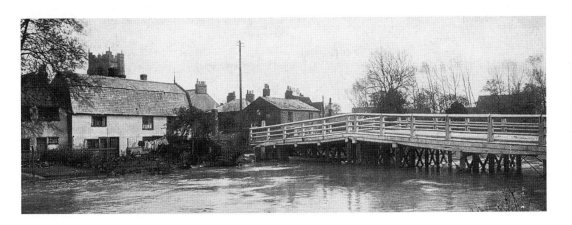

Brundon Mill, Sudbury.

August 26 1661: The Chamberlain to take off the gates of the town, at the ends of the town, and make thereof money for the repair of Ballingdon Bridge.

From the *Ipswich Journal*:

1757 September: Ballingdon Bridge is ripped up on the Suffolk side and for three weeks impassable for carriages and horses which had to go across the common.
1761 August: Traffic at Sudbury disrupted again as Ballingdon Bridge is broken up, to be repaired on the Essex side.
1767 August: Ballingdon Bridge is under repair on both sides creating six and a half weeks of diversion via the common lands.

opposite above The mill and bridge at Brundon, a beauty spot north of the town. This was the place where the river could be forded by people coming into Suffolk from Essex before Ballingdon bridge was built.

opposite below The bridge on the Croft giving quick access to the meadows from the town centre.

Traffic using the common lands would have crossed over the Mancroft Bridge, a few yards upstream and used by cattle to pass from one part of the common to another, and then pass through the ford at the mill pool. They were then faced with a very steep hill at Salter's Hall. In the early nineteenth century the road builder Macadam was called in to alter the gradient, not just here but on Ballingdon Hill as well.

It is not clear when the stone bridge was finally abandoned and replaced with a timber structure. Brewer's map of Sudbury dated 1714 clearly shows a timber bridge similar to those which existed at Rodbridge, Henny, Bures and other crossing points along the valley. The introduction of a concrete bridge in 1910 gave much needed stability but nobody could have foreseen the increase and weight of traffic it was subsequently to carry. A new bridge, opened in 2003, is elegant and modern yet seen from the meadows it blends in with its surroundings and has more than a hint of the traditional timber bridges of the Stour.

chapter six

Seventeenth and eighteenth centuries

Decline of the Cloth Trade

The peak of Sudbury's medieval prosperity was reached with the advent of the Tudors but towards the close of Elizabeth's reign the cloth trade in Sudbury was in decline. The woollens were being replaced by the 'new draperies' being produced in Holland and Yorkshire. They used greater quantities of wool but were lighter and stronger. Suffolk clothiers could compete but were hindered by the growing influences of the London merchants to the finishing and marketing of their products. There was a reluctance to change but Sudbury and Long Melford continued to manufacture bays and says into the eighteenth century.

In 1660 an attempt was made to boost the declining industry by an Act of Parliament which ordered that all corpses were to be buried in woollen shrouds, the penalty for non compliance being £5. Through most of the seventeenth century it was a depressing time in Sudbury. There was much poverty and very little to lighten the gloom. The puritanic approach to life and religion did nothing to improve matters. During the civil war Sudbury supported the Parliamentarians, but the town seems not to have been affected unduly. Large numbers did leave the district to find a new life in America, others moved up to Yorkshire where the cloth trade was flourishing.

The Gainsboroughs

In 1657 a certain Robert Gainsborough was apprenticed to John Thompson, a saymaker of Sudbury. Ten years later he married Frances Maynard at Little Cornard church and together they produced four sons and three daughters. He was involved in the manufacturing and merchandising of fine worsteds and funery crêpe and bays and says whereby he founded the family fortune. He became one of the twenty-four capital burgesses on the town council and was made chief constable of Sudbury, in which capacity he was often accused of

These decorative cast-iron screens protect the ground floor windows of the little cottage in Friar's Street where Gainsborough lived and his daughters were born.

being too lenient towards the ever growing body of Nonconformists in the town. He was particularly defensive of the Great Meeting House in Friar's Street where later members of his family would become leading lights.

He died in 1716 and was buried in St Gregory's churchyard a wealthy and respected man. His eldest surviving child was his daughter Susannah who had married a clothier Abraham Griggs in 1689. They purchased a large property in Cross Street part of which they made their home while the remainder was used as business premises and became known as The Warehouse. Their son Thomas Griggs, after a faltering start, made a huge fortune in the bunting industry where he not only cornered the market but became almost the sole supplier of bunting to the Navy.

Susannah's brother Thomas carried on his father's business, he had married Sarah Peto in 1702. She was the daughter of Samuel Peto, head of the Friar's Street Meeting House. She died in childbirth but he remarried, this time a lady of fortune Elizabeth Fenn. The Fenns lived in Ballingdon and they were cloth makers, merchants and bankers and, by the nineteenth century were also into brick-making at Middleton. Elizabeth was the mother of eight children, only one of whom would maintain connections with Sudbury although most of his business would be conducted in London. His name was John and the woman he married was Mary English of Saffron Walden, heiress to a large fortune.

Susannah's second brother John did not inherit his father's business acumen and tried his hand at various things. He has been described as a milliner, a clothier and a crêpe-maker. He married Mary Burrough at St Andrew's church, Great Cornard. Her parents owned the Christopher Inn in Sepulchre Street which may have influenced him into purchasing two properties immediately opposite. One of them is believed to have been The Black Horse tavern about which little is known. The other was known as Guibler's which we know was owned by Thomas Godfrey in 1645, Bernard Carter in 1664, and John Thompson in 1716 who sold it to John Gainsborough for £230 in 1722.

John Gainsborough linked the two properties behind a red brick classical façade, the first time such a thing was done in Sudbury, and it started a new fashion. It introduced brickwork to the streets of Sudbury, until then every house in the town was timber-framed. It must have impressed the locals considerably and it sums up his character beautifully, not enough money to go the whole hog but enough to create a lasting impression of wealth, good taste and high fashion. It probably cost him every penny he had. There is no doubt that he would have had to employ an architect as there is so much subtle detail, for example the two-toned bricks and the clever use of headers and stretchers. The simple Doric door case, the elegant segment headed windows, probably the first sash windows to be seen in the town, the decorative brick aprons under the first floor windows and that final touch of a slight projection – just two bricks in width – at each end of the façade, all add up to a building of distinction.

He would have seen houses like this in Spitalfields when visiting London but there is also a great similarity with Belchamp Hall, the seat of the Raymonds over the border in Essex.

The Raymonds were friends of the Gainsboroughs and their house was erected in 1720 and Robert Taylor senior was their architect. It is fortunate that the public has access to John Gainsborough's house because once one has passed over the threshold its origins are immediately apparent. The narrow hallway represents the passageway between the two timber-framed properties. On the left is the parlour with exposed timberwork including a sixteenth-century doorway. There is also a restored open brick fireplace but John Gainsborough had concealed all this to make an elegant plain room. What we see today is a result of the restoration of the building in 1959 when it was thought necessary to reveal the true age of the house. Perhaps it would have been better to record the features and restore it back to its eighteenth-century appearance.

Across the hallway is the dining room, very much as the Gainsboroughs knew it, with a beautiful moulded timber ceiling. The fireplace is missing but there is an alcove with seventeenth-century painted decoration and an eighteenth-century Gothic surround. The back of the house was remodelled in the eighteenth century and the finest features are the upper and lower bow rooms. The lower has triple Gothic windows reaching to the floor. When these rooms were added a new and elegant staircase was introduced. The upper rooms at the rear were remodelled and large windows inserted to accommodate silk weaving looms in the early nineteenth century when the house was annexed to the adjoining one-time silk factory in Weaver's Lane.

The house today serves as a museum and art gallery to commemorate the fact that Thomas Gainsborough, the painter and son of John, was born in this house

A few yards behind Gainsborough's cottage is this splendid mansion, The Red House, now a home for retired persons. It is set in charming gardens and when it was built had spectacular meadow views.

in 1727. Here, it is claimed, is the largest collection of his works under one roof. Exhibitions of other artist's work are regularly held in the well-lit gallery and the house draws visitors from all over the world. The garden is enchanting and is often the setting for open-air displays of art.

Thomas Gainsborough the Painter

Thomas was baptised at the Great Meeting House in Friar's Street on 14 May 1727 and showed a talent for drawing at an early age. He was educated at Sudbury Grammar School where his maternal uncle, Humphrey Burrough, was schoolmaster and curate at St Gregory's church. With help from his uncle, Thomas, who lived in Friar's Street, was sent up to London to study as a pupil of Hubert Gravelot, a French draughtsman and engraver in 1740. Five years later at the age of eighteen he opened his own studio in Hatton Garden.

A year later he was introduced to and married Margaret Burr at Dr Keith's Mayfair Chapel, a somewhat notorious place renowned for clandestine marriages. Almost certainly Margaret was pregnant but the child died young and was buried at St Andrew's Holborn on 1 March 1747.

Thomas returned to Sudbury with his wife a short time after and they were living in a cottage on the corner of Bullocks Lane in Friar's Street when their second child Mary was born and baptised at All Saints church on 3 February 1748. Another daughter, Margaret, was born in the same house and baptised at St Gregory's on 21 August 1751. These two girls would become world famous through the portraits their father painted of them throughout their lives. The most beautiful and haunting being 'The Painter's Daughters Chasing a Butterfly' that hangs in the National Gallery.

While living in Friar's Street he was commissioned to paint the double portrait of Robert Andrews and his wife Frances Carter. The painting shows the couple in their park at Auberies on the edge of Sudbury with the sweeping

The garden of The Red House has a serpentine wall and a gazebo from which to watch the barges go to the quay and back. Serpentine, or 'crinkle crankle', walls provide sheltered bays for fruit. Until recently these were usually only found in East Anglia.

landscape of the Stour Valley behind them that shows the tower of All Saints where they were married in November 1748. It also depicts the rear of Ballingdon Hall, the chalk pit in Middleton Road and the distant fields above Great Cornard. It was an early masterpiece the like of which he was never to paint again and that too hangs in the National Gallery in London as does his painting of Cornard Wood, also painted while living in this cottage. In a letter he writes that he painted it from sketches he did while at school that his mother had kept. There are some more of his pictures from this Sudbury period in the collection at Gainsborough's House.

The family moved to Ipswich in 1752 and on to Bath seven years later by which time his reputation was made. He was a founder member of the Royal Academy with whom he quarrelled in 1773 over the hanging of his pictures. He settled in London in 1774 taking a tenancy of the west wing of Schomberg House in Pall Mall. After exhibiting full-length portraits of George III and Queen Charlotte at the Academy he became the unofficial court painter receiving commissions from other members of the royal family.

In 1784 he quarrelled again with the Academy about the hanging of his pictures and withdrew his exhibits. He died on 2 August 1788 of a cancer in his neck and is buried in Kew churchyard. His quarrels with the Royal Academy were not petty. Many of his exhibits were commissions to be hung in a special place at a certain height and painted to meet those conditions. He simply wanted his pictures viewed accordingly.

These are just the bare facts, volumes have been written about his life and art but he was undoubtedly a genius, original, always experimenting, a great figure in the history of English art and, above all, a Sudburian.

Margaret Burr, his wife, was an attractive woman and the wonderful portrait he painted of her in the 1780s suggests that she retained her attractiveness through middle age. She was of Scottish descent and had hinted that she was of royal blood.

We know that she received an annuity of £200 per annum from Henry, Duke of Beaufort, and it was assumed that he was her natural father. More recent investigations seem to suggest that he was acting on behalf of Frederick, Prince of Wales. What has not been cleared up is how they met. The late Miss Holden of Trinity Lodge in School Street was a direct descendant of Robert Andrews, she not only told me how that famous double portrait was passed around the family and once hung in her father's house at 58 Friar's Street, but that it was understood in the family that Robert Andrews introduced Gainsborough to his wife, 'knowing that a wife with an annuity was a very valuable asset for a man following so precarious a profession as a painter of faces'.

If it is true that Andrews had a house in Grosvenor Square at the time when Gainsborough was in London, the Mayfair Chapel was but a stone's throw away. Small wonder then that he painted such a stunning portrait for Mr and Mrs Robert Andrews, perhaps he owed them a favour.

The Navigation of the River

There is an item in the Town Books of 1634 in connection with the accounts of the late Mayor Daniel Biatt, ' Spent at The Chequer in wyne with Mr Doctor Warren and Mr Spenser, when we did meete aboute making the river navigable, 2s.'

In 1628 Arnold Spenser had been granted Letters Patent by King Charles I to make the River Stour navigable. Six years later he was having a drink at The Chequer Inn, the site of the present town hall, with the mayor and still talking about it. There are some who think he may have made a start but there is no clear evidence to support it. Certainly he had in 1618 made part of the River Ouse suitable for barge traffic.

In 1705 during the reign of Queen Anne, an Act of Parliament was passed to make the river navigable from Sudbury to Manningtree. It was thought that by doing so it would be very good for trade, especially for the conveyance of coal and other goods. According to the Act the mayor and aldermen of Sudbury and ten gentlemen of the town, Thomas Carter, Roger Scarlin, John Parish, Robert Girling, Henry Crossman, Robert Sparrow, Thomas Hall, Thomas Firmin, Daniel Hasel and Thomas Robinson were appointed as 'undertakers'.

The 'undertakers' were given the necessary powers for making the river navigable. If in the course of doing so there were disputes over riparian rights then a hundred commissioners were appointed to act as referees from which nine could make a quorum with full powers. The names of the commissioners are all listed, over thirty of whom were titled. It was expected that the 'undertakers' would start work on 24 June 1708 and complete the task within five years to the day. If they failed the commissioners could appoint others to complete the work. Brewer's map of Sudbury, dated 1714, shows the quay with two warehouses.

The Act gave them powers to construct new channels, locks, and any other works necessary to enable barges, boats, lighters etc., to have passage for the full twenty-four miles between the two towns. In 1780 a further Act had to be passed to amend the first and to appoint new commissioners because almost all those named on the original Act were dead and no provision had been made for replacements.

Piers and wharves were constructed at villages along the route to serve the numerous mills and maltings and at Sudbury a special half-mile cut was made from Friar's Meadows to the Ballingdon Grove Brickworks and chalk pit. There were fifteen locks to be negotiated by the horse-drawn barges and because the towpath switched from one side to another a horse would have to cross the river thirty-three times on the whole trip from Sudbury to Brantham.

Sudbury became an inland river-port and the navigation was used for transporting all kinds of heavy goods. One list shows, 'Oil in pipes, Oil in Hogsheads, Pitch in Barrels, Tallow, Iron and Lead by the cwt, Nails in bags, Crates of Glass, Firkins of Butter, and Grindstones for Mills'. This list is dated 1750.

above In Edwardian days pleasure trips by barge to Bures were a feature of the summer months. The barge in this picture has just arrived at Bures.

opposite above The Sudbury quay warehouse built in 1791 and before the additions of 1984. It was purchased in 1977 by the Sudbury Dramatic Society and formally opened as a theatre by Max Wall in 1981.

opposite below Another view of the quay with work in progress. A second warehouse called The Granary is now the headquarters of the River Stour Trust.

In the nineteenth century huge amounts of grain were being moved, barley for the many maltings along the valley, then lime, chalk and coal. From Sudbury thousands of bricks were taken to Manningtree and switched to Thames barges for Chelsea Wharf in London where much of South Kensington was being built following the Great Exhibition of 1851. A 'gang of barges' (two barges) was expected to take twelve hours from Sudbury to Cattawade Bridge and fourteen hours on the return. In Middleton Road is a row of cottages built for the bargees who worked for Allen's brickworks.

The arrival of the railway in 1849 and its extension to Cambridge in 1865 became a real threat to the Navigation and eventually led to its demise and the company went into voluntary liquidation in 1913.

There can be no doubt that the Navigation was an enormous boon because in spite of some negative reports from visitors, who were apt to compare it with St Edmundsbury and Ipswich, the eighteenth-century buildings throughout the town show there was in fact a fair amount of prosperity. Towards the end of the century a new industry was introduced which flourishes still – silk weaving.

The River Stour Trust was formed in 1968 as a campaigning body to conserve and maintain the right of navigation on the river and is committed to restoring through navigation between Sudbury and the estuary. They have done much work and a visit to their headquarters at the restored granary at The Quay can be very enlightening.

chapter seven

Nineteenth century

Silk Weaving

The Spitalfields Act of 1774, which gave Justices power to fix wages for the London weavers, was partly the reason for manufacturers looking outside London to set up branches. The increasing use of coal fires in the city was also causing pollution that could infiltrate into the workshops and threaten damage to the silk. They looked towards East Anglia because of the weaving skills available and the relatively smoke-free atmosphere compared with that of London.

By paying wages based on piece-work rates, which amounted to only two thirds of those fixed for London, the Suffolk weaver was still able to earn more than he could make in the woollen industry.

To accommodate this new industry a large area in the vicinity of St Gregory's church was cleared and specially designed terraces of house were erected. They were three storeys high with large windows on the first floor to light the loom. The very first terrace was Gooseberry Row off North Street behind the Cavendish Cottages and they faced an open field called Windmill Field. These were followed by Church Walk and The Croft and then the whole of Gregory Street. These early terraces were designed with connecting doors on the first floor so that the employer could enter the first house and inspect the looms through the whole terrace and re-emerge from the last house. Later, when the trade was factory orientated, the doors were disposed with.

Later terraces appeared in Cross Street and Ballingdon and a second terrace was built on Windmill Field called Inkerman Row. The remainder of the field was developed to form New Street and Prince Street. Eventually, because of lack of space within the town, it was necessary for them to build outside. A weaving community appeared on the Melford Road, until then a country road, and it was provided with shops and a pub. Another was built on the Bulmer Road called Batt Hall (after the brick batts made at the nearby brickfield), again with a shop and pub, and a third in East Street.

After the Spitalfields Act of 1774 the silk industry was set up in Sudbury where weaving skills were available at cheaper rates than London and the air was cleaner. Terraces of three-storey houses with large first floor windows to light the loom were built by the manufacturers for their workers. Many of these were demolished in the 1960s, especially around Gregory Street and The Croft. The houses here were in Church Walk, just off The Croft

Surviving weavers houses are now much sought after, such as this terrace in East Street

Apart from home weavers some manufacturers set up small factories that provided better training for the workers and also prevented pilfering. In 1844 there were 600 looms in the town employing 300 men and probably the same number of women. By 1851 the number employed in the industry had risen to 852. The early products are described as 'silks, velvets, and satins' but from the beginning Sudbury was concerned with high class fabrics of a specialist nature and still is to this day.

Between 1895 and 1905 the power loom was introduced and under the factory system familiar names appeared which are with us still. Stephen Walters, the oldest silk manufacturing firm in Great Britain, Vanners and Fennell (the amalgamation of two firms) and in 1903, The Gainsborough Silk Weaving Co., started by Reginald Warner. These factories still prosper and between them produce fabric of world renown and Sudbury is now the largest silk manufacturing centre in Britain, if not in Europe.

Damask from Sudbury hangs on the walls of the National Gallery, The Tate Gallery, The Wallace Collection and The Maritime Museum. Curtains from the Gainsborough Silk Weaving Co. hang in The Houses of Parliament, Apsley House, Clarence House, Marlborough House, St James Palace and numerous National Trust properties and embassies throughout the world.

Stephen Walters produced the silk linings for the Queen's coronation robes, the silk fabric for Princess Diana's wedding dress and numerous other royal commissions. These factories carry on a tradition that first made the town prosperous seven centuries ago when Sudbury woollens were famous throughout Europe.

From *A Frenchman in England* by Francois De La Rochefoucauld 1784

'On our arrival at Sudbury we had breakfast and then sent for a manufacturer who told us a little about the trade of the town and its population. There is one remarkable thing for which the most competent authorities would find it difficult to give a proper account. Why is the population of the towns so different in regard to the class of people who live distributed in each town? Why are some towns inhabited only by the dregs of the people and by ne'er-do-wells?

I must recollect that I am in England, where the nobility and the gentry, who two or three months of the year are in the capital, are evenly distributed through all the counties round all the towns. The country around Sudbury is pleasant enough, the hills and valleys provide agreeable prospects, and yet the town and its neighbourhood are inhabited only by people without any fortune, by smugglers, bankrupts and the like. It is a misfortune for which I cannot account, but it is an established fact that there is not a decent man in the place.

There is a considerable trade in wool and silk stuffs. The latter are all for the London market, and the money being invested by merchants from the Capital who get the work done at the lowest prices. There are about a hundred looms at work. The number of woolen looms is larger; I do not know how many there are, as the manufacturer could not tell us. The cloth is course and thick, a kind of double serge suitable for being made into dresses for women of the lower classes. It is made in lengths of twenty-seven to forty yards, a yard being 3ft.

The trade of the town is as large as it can be, I mean that all hands are engaged in it, and even fresh hands would find work there. During the period of the American War the trade declined and sank almost to nothing, but now it has recovered its former vigour. However they say as regards Camlet and calendered stuffs, which they make in large quantities, France is beginning to be a serious rival.

The workman's wage is from twelve to sixteen shillings a week, a shilling being worth twenty-four sous. The rent of land on the outskirts of the town is twelve shillings an acre.'

Oddly enough when Defoe passed through Sudbury in 1722 he said much the same thing,' the town is very populous and very poor ... the number of poor was almost ready to eat up the rich...' I can add myself, in this vein, that when my family moved into Ballingdon from Hertfordshire in 1941 our neighbour, Mrs Emma Felton who was then in her late seventies and ran a grocery shop with her daughter, said emphatically to a customer, 'As for Sudbury, there's not a gentleman in the town and hasn't been for years'. I later realised that what she meant was that no titled person lived within the borough boundary. Probably the circumstances were the same during the Frenchman's visit, but his admiration for the nobility must have received a severe jolt five years later when his countrymen turned on them with such ferocity.

Town Improvements

In 1826 an Act of Parliament was passed for Paving, Lighting, Cleansing, Watching, Watering, and Improving the Town and Borough of Sudbury in

Two mansions were built in Sudbury during the eighteenth century. This house on Market Hill was built by the Revd Henry Crossman for his daughter in 1768 when she married Edward Green of Lawford Hall. It has been a bank now for over a century.

Suffolk. A further Act was passed in 1842 to enlarge, amend and alter the powers and provisions of the former Act. The borough council through these Acts was given power to raise the funds through the rates to thoroughly improve the town.

The town was in dire need of improvement, not just the centre either, there was also much that needed doing in the streets of the old town beyond the Market Hill. There were no pavements in Cross Street or Church Street and some houses projected more into the street than others, and in North Street as well. The congestion caused by encroachment on the Market Hill has been mentioned but to this must be added the dangerous road conditions in Stour Street where there was an extremely precipitous hill just past Salter's Hall and there was a serious problem with traffic both ways at Cornard End in Borehamgate. One phrase in the original Act states that in future all houses in Sudbury shall be built upright, for until then almost all the buildings in Sudbury were timber-framed with overhanging first floors. There would be no sentiment. allowed, and no matter whose house it was, or who lived in it, if it offended the new great scheme then it had to go.

Every building or piece of land affected was listed in the second Act, so were the owners and the occupiers. Thus we see that Edmund Stedman of Belle Vue lost his stable and brew house in Newton Road by Cornard End. The twelve houses which stretched across the road forming Cornard End in Borehamgate were removed, so were four houses round the church and two in Chequer Lane. The George Inn had its medieval front made flush and was given a façade in brick. Any part of the churchyard at St Peter's which extended more than 10ft from the church was taken to be part of the footway.

Thirteen houses were removed or refronted in Cross Street, three houses, a stable and one large bay window in Church Street. That last item must surely

Not such a happy ending for Belle Vue pictured here in 1820. It was built by Nathaniel Burrough, a retired city grocer and cousin of Thomas Gainsborough the painter. Sadly the house was demolished in the nineteenth century and replaced by another.

This picture postcard dated 1905 shows the splendid Corn Exchange, now the library, and the Queen Anne-style Barclays Bank.

have been a shop window. All of this to allow the streets to be paved, but as we can see today, those pavements are extremely narrow.

Mr Thomas Ginn, a local builder who lived in Borehamgate, was commissioned to build a new town hall in the fashionable Greek style on the site of The Exchequer Inn. He produced a most elegant building in white Ballingdon brick with a stuccoed front of three bays with a pedimented centre on a pair of coupled Ionic columns. In the pediment were the arms of the borough. There was a courtroom for the Quarterly Assizes and the Mayor's Parlour on the ground floor. A central staircase hall led up to the Assembly Room that fills the width of the building. At the rear the old and impressive entrance to the gaol, which held the prisoners overnight before the assizes, has been skilfully adapted to serve the modern extensions. The cost of the new town hall was a little over £2,000 and it was completed in 1828.

Two years later sentiment was not considered when the sixteenth-century Moot Hall was sold to the commissioners of the Act for £300 so that it might be pulled down and the site laid into the public road. In the space between the doomed houses fronting St Peter's and the Moot Hall was a circle of posts where the Corn Market was held and due notice was given that the space would not be available in the not too distant future for that purpose. A company was formed and approaches were made to purchase The Coffee House Inn where the proprietor had recently died.

Most market towns in the eighteenth century had a coffee house where the locals would meet to exchange news, read the newspapers and transact business. They were respectable places and the last landlord in Sudbury was a Mr Hitchacock who is buried in St Gregory's churchyard. It says a lot for the respectability of such houses that he is described on his tombstone as 'Late

Landlord of the Coffee House Inn'. The new Corn Exchange Company purchased the inn from his widow and for a year or two on Market Days it served as a Corn Market. It was demolished in 1839 and the site cleared for a new Corn Exchange

The architect they engaged to design the building was H.E. Kendall who was very busy at Wimpole Hall in Cambridgeshire. This meant that he was a long time producing the plans and it was not completed until 1841. The façade has echoes of the stable block at Wimpole Hall which he had designed in a baroque style in red brick. At Sudbury he chose stuccoed brick but the baroque influence is apparent and the plan is like a Georgian church with nave and aisles. Inside, the columns are cast iron and there is a clerestory where daylight, essential for selling corn, pours in through attractive and dainty skylights. The façade has three tall bays with giant Tuscan columns soaring up to support the entablature which projects and carries wheat sheaves. Above everything is a statue group of 'The Resting Reapers'.

In the tympanum above the door is some energetic baroque cast iron while the tall, round-headed windows on either side have a dainty network of tracery. The scale is perfect for the site and inside the keen eye may notice that the façade is slightly curved to follow the line of the street. Also inside, on a keystone above the central window, is the architect's name and the date, 1841.

It is shocking to know that this building was threatened with demolition in the 1960s but a strong fight by local people, assisted by several preservation groups, gained a reprieve. The county council stepped in and converted the building into a branch library. Their architect, Jack Digby, floated mezzanine floors like galleries into the aisles and all is light, bright and cheerful as a modern library should be.

By the time this building was completed all the houses backing on to the church were demolished and Sudbury had regained Elizabeth de Burgh's great open space. For many years, until the advent of the motorcar, it was used for all kinds of parades and public events as well as the market. That was the original intention but today the south side is part of a busy main through road and as long as that is the case the people of Sudbury cannot use their civic square to the full.

In 1834 there was a by-election in Sudbury and the hustings were erected on the Market Hill on the site of the old Moot Hall. Next door to Lloyds Bank, where Westminster Bank is now, was the Swan Inn with its balcony above a bay window. Staying in that inn was a reporter for *The Morning Post* sent down from London to cover the by-election and his name was Charles Dickens. The balcony was an excellent viewpoint from which to observe and hear the candidate's speeches and the heckling voter's jeers and cheers. Everything he witnessed was used in his serialised book *Pickwick Papers* where Sudbury wears a thin disguise as Eatanswill. The Swan appears as The Peacock and the Town Arms, headquarters of The Blues and where their procession was formed, has been identified as Sudbury's Rose and Crown. Unfortunately neither has survived but the house with the tiled roof and leaden gutter from which Mrs Pott and Mr Winkle witnessed the election is now Lloyds Bank.

The north side of Market Hill in the late eighteenth century. The Moot Hall is far left and houses in front of the church are far right. The Black Boy has not yet acquired its Georgian façade and neither has E.W. King next door, shown here with a gable.

At that time Sudbury returned two members to Parliament and the town was fast gaining a reputation for bribery and corruption at the polls. The by-election was caused by the death of one of the members, the Rt Hon. M.A. Taylor. It caused a sensation because the two candidates, Sir Edward Barnes (Tory) and Mr Bagshaw (Whig) polled an equal number of votes and the casting vote of the mayor in favour of Barnes decided the outcome. However, at the General Election a few months later Mr Bagshaw got his revenge and unseated Barnes.

It was the General Election of 1841 which saw huge quantities of gold brought into the town, £4,500 in total, for distribution amongst the electors as inducements to vote. One of the two members returned was David Ochterlony Dyce-Sombre who by descent was a Eurasian. Because of his dark colour the local paper quipped:

> Most gracious Mistress, we have done our best
> And send a man no blacker than the rest

The other successful candidate was Frederick Villiers, but neither was to stay long as members for the borough. Because of the quite unconcealed corruption witnessed at the election a petition was lodged against them and they were unseated. An enquiry was set up which led to an Act of Parliament being passed by which Sudbury was disenfranchised on 29 July 1844.

Lighting the Town with Gas

On 27 January 1836, the mayor of Sudbury, Robert Ransom, chaired a meeting in the new town hall to discuss the lighting of the town. It would be wrong to assume that there was no street lighting until then because there was a very limited number of oil lanterns, mounted on wall brackets, about the town. They were privately owned and one has survived outside a house in Cross Street, although it was later adapted for gas. At the mayor's meeting it was resolved, 'That in the opinion of this meeting it is expedient to form a Company to light the town with Gas'.

A Company was formed immediately 'under the name, title, or firm of the Sudbury Gas and Coke Company, for the express object and purpose of manufacturing and producing inflammable air or gas from coal, oil, or other materials, and of supplying therewith the Town of Sudbury, in the County of Suffolk'.

Amongst the first subscribers to the company are the names of the town's elite, William Cole Adams, George W. Andrews, John Bridgman, Stephen Brown, John Burkitt, Richard Gainsborough Dupont, William Goldsmith, Charles Harding, William Wood Humphry, William Doubleday King, Robert Ransom, Edmund Stedman (Belle Vue) and John Sikes (East House).

The company supplied the town with eighty public lamps at thirty shillings each per annum. The gas works was sited on Nonsuch Meadow in Quay Lane, off Friar's Street.

The railway had not yet reached Sudbury so the quayside site for the gas works was essential. Coal was brought to Sudbury by the river barges which made it necessary for the company to have their own cutting at the quay so that the coal could be offloaded on site. In their centenary brochure it states, 'It is interesting to note that a small experimental plant for the manufacture of Coal Gas is said to have been installed in King Street previous to that date (1836); but this was in no way connected with the Gas Company, and authoritative particulars concerning its existence are not available'.

The commissioners of the Sudbury Paving and Lighting Act had a contract with the company for lighting the town with gas for thirty years, subsequently reduced to twenty. The company engaged the services of George and James Malam to erect a gas works and plant because they had already done so at Bury St Edmunds, Newmarket and Ely.

Eventually street lighting went over to electricity but the gas lamp posts, minus their lanterns, were not removed from the pavements until the late 1950s, a pair outside St Peter's were still in place in 1974. A contract between Sudbury Town Council and the Empire Company for carrying out a system of electric lighting in the town was signed and sealed in May 1904, the company being under a bond for £2,000 to commence the work within six months.

The Sudbury Town Lands Act 1838

Sudbury's greatest and most treasured possession is its Common Lands which encompass the town on three sides. It comes as a surprise to many to learn that only about one third is ancient and original; Portmanscroft, (now called Freemens Little Common and Great Common) and Kingsmere (now Kingsmarsh), which total approxiamately forty-one acres. These were lands outside the ditch which became more accessible when the bridge was built in around 1180. Portmanscroft was the pasture immediately backing onto the newly formed Croft Street, the street took its name from the Croft and it has only been called Cross Street since the seventeenth century. Kingsmere was part of the marshland through which the raised causeway crossed and it backs on to Ballingdon Street.

To these was added Little Fulling Pit meadow to the north which brought the Common Land acreage to fifty-one and a half acres in the eighteenth century. A further seventy-three acres was acquired in the nineteenth century but not until Parliament passed the Sudbury Town Lands Act of 1838.

The freemen grazed their cattle on the Common Land through the summer months while the grass was growing. For the remaining six months, after crops had been gathered in, they had the right to turn their cattle on to neighbouring fields to feed off stubble, loose grain and any other residue, even though they never owned the land. These were known as 'shackage rights'. As long as the freemen had shackage rights the landowners could not develop their land.

Although the population had risen the town had not expanded beyond the parameters set in the fourteenth century. There was nothing except market gardens beyond North Street, the only houses in Melford Road were Colneys Almshouse opposite North Meadows and the notorious King's Arms Inn at Holgate towards Rodbridge. This was the haunt of highwaymen and thugs who would know in advance if a traveller with money or valuables was soon to pass, thanks to their contacts in the Sudbury town centre inns. Holgate House stands on the site today.

The fields of Wood Hall came right down to Girling Street and East Street had houses for only 100 yards or so. Newton Road and Cornard Road were undeveloped and between them sat Nathaniel Borough's mansion, Belle Vue. The Sudbury Town Lands Act allowed landowners to redeem shackage rights by exchanging them for land or cash or sometimes both. This enabled the freemen to consolidate their lands with the purchase of Great Fulling Pit Meadow and North Meadows while Harp Close Meadow in Waldingfield Road provided upland grazing. They had the use of Friar's Meadow but this did not form part of the Common Lands until the mid-twentieth century.

With restrictions lifted the town immediately began expanding and some of the first buildings to be erected on the newly available sites were for the silk weavers. The brickyards at Ballingdon and Chilton had difficulty in keeping up with the demand for bricks as the villas for the rising middle classes progressed along Melford Road. They were built on the high ground above the more modest terraces just across the road. Brick terraces were also built to replace the houses demolished under the Town Improvement Act in Church Street, and Cross Street.

The late John Wardman's book, *Sudbury Common Lands*, must be read to fully appreciate the history of Sudbury's most precious asset. From the thirteenth century the Common Lands were under the stewardship of Sudbury's mayor and corporation on behalf of the freemen. A high court judgement in 1897 vested the lands with the Charity Commission on behalf of the freemen with local trustees in charge of the management. However, since 1987 it was ordered that the charity should be managed for the benefit of the inhabitants of Sudbury.

The Workhouse

The first Sudbury workhouse was established following an Act of 1702 in the reign of Queen Anne for 'erecting Hospitals and Workhouses within the Town of Sudbury, in the County of Suffolk, for the better imploying and maintaining the Poor thereof'.

The preamble to the Act States:

> Whereas it is found by experience, that the Poor of the Borough and Town of Sudbury in the County of Suffolk, do multiply and Idleness and Debauchery, amongst the meaner sort, doth daily increase, for want of Workhouses to set them to work, with a sufficient Authority to compel them thereto, as well to the Charge of the Inhabitants, and Grief of the charitable and honest householders of the said Town, as the great Distress of the Poor themselves; for which sufficient Redress hath not yet been provided...

The Act grants the authority for a Court of Guardians to be set up comprising the mayor, aldermen and eight other persons to be elected by the rate-payers of Sudbury's three parishes. They were responsible for collecting the Poor Rate, for distributing relief to the poor and for the establishing and administering of a workhouse. To this end they purchased the remaining portion of St Gregory's College which had for years been a private house.

Records for this period are scant but it would seem that there was a strict regime designed to keep the inmates busy and only a little better than the prisons of the day. Whole families could be consigned to the workhouse but at least they were allowed to work outside so that there was always a glimmer of hope that one day they could re-establish themselves in the community. The Sudbury workhouse was for the Sudbury poor, other villages had their own 'poor house' with differing degrees of hardship but in small communities there was also a certain amount of compassion, after all, there but for the grace of God go I.

All of this was to change with The Poor Law Act of 1834 introduced by the Whig Government whereby groups of parishes were combined into 'unions' each with one large workhouse. Outdoor work was denied to the inmates and the strict regulations for the running of the workhouse was vested in the Poor Law Commissioners. The regulations were to make life inside the institution so harsh that poverty and sickness among the poor was treated as a crime. The Sudbury Union covered twenty-four Suffolk parishes and eighteen from Essex and plans for the building of a new workhouse for four to five hundred inmates were drawn up and John Brown of Norwich was appointed as architect.

The workhouse was administered by an elected Board of Guardians, four from Sudbury and two from Long Melford and one from each of the remaining parishes within the union. The old Sudbury workhouse was purchased for £500 but continued to be run by the old Court of Guardians while work began on the new buildings in 1835. The incomplete building was damaged by fire in 1836 and an enquiry failed to establish the cause. It was finally completed the following year at a cost of £10,000 and the last remnants of Simon's College were demolished, except for a single gateway into the churchyard.

Public opinion was divided concerning the Act and the treatment of inmates bitterly criticised, especially the separation of married couples from each other and from their children. As for children, they would be apprenticed to tradesmen when old enough and sent out into the world without reference or regard to their parents.

A real friend to the poor locally was George William Fulcher, the son of a tailor, who was born in the town in 1795. He followed in his father's trade but later was better known as a printer and publisher of the annual *Ladies Pocket Memorandum Book*, circulated nationwide. He was prominent in local affairs and a staunch Tory. He was a JP and became mayor four times in 1846, 1848, 1852 and 1854. He died a year later leaving an incomplete manuscript of the life of Gainsborough which his son completed. Although he became a guardian of the union he was bitterly opposed to the Poor Law Act and wrote a long poem, 'The Village Paupers', which was a sustained attack on it. Parts appeared in the *Ladies Pocket Memorandum Book* between 1840 and1844 and was eventually published complete in 1845. A shortened version, edited by E.A. Goodwyn was published in 1981 complete with Fulcher's own notes. A deeply harrowing poem it is nevertheless worth reading to get a full insight into the plight of the poor and the appalling arrogance and insensitivity which the Poor Law Amendment Act engendered.

Fulcher is buried in St Gregory's churchyard and has a monument a few yards from the porch and within sight of the workhouse he so much despised.

The workhouse was enlarged in 1849 at a cost of £4,000 to accommodate a total capacity of 422 inmates although the maximum was only ever about 250. There was a constant trickle of tramps and vagrants who were allowed to stay overnight and given a meal in exchange for a task of some kind but they were obliged to move on next day. In 1929 the Board of Guardians was abolished and their responsibility was taken over by West Suffolk County Council.

In 1948 the Sudbury workhouse was placed under the West Suffolk Hospital Management Committee and re-named Walnuttree Hospital. It took years of determined work and effort to remove the stigma attached to the buildings. This was the year when the National Health Service Act was introduced by the Labour Party and with it came the National Assistance Act which finally saw the last of the old Poor Law.

Today the hospital has a reputation second to none with regard to the treat- ment of its patients and the running of its out-patients departments. At the time of writing there are plans for a new hospital at Chilton which will replace Walnuttree. Ironically it will probably release land for redevelopment with stunning views over the Common Lands which only the rich will be able to afford.

St Leonards Hospital in Newton Road was built in 1867 with two wards and an operating theatre. It was supported by voluntary subscriptions and the residue of Colney's Charity. It was enlarged with a maternity wing but has since been closed down. Another small isolation hospital with twelve beds was set up off Waldingfield Road in 1912 by the corporation but that too was closed many years ago.

The Arrival of the Railway

The Stour Valley Railway from Marks Tey reached Sudbury in 1849 and the terminus was just behind Cornard End at the commencement of the newly constructed Great Eastern Road. The large meadow behind the south side of the Market Hill, where Mr Thomas Ginn had recently built a fine terrace of houses named Bank Buildings, was marked out with twenty-two building plots. 'Very eligibly situated close by the Sudbury Station, and near the Market Hill in the centre of that flourishing and improving town' said the poster advertising the auction to be held at the Rose and Crown Hotel. It goes on:

From the proximity of this land to the Station and the Town it is eminently adapted for the erection of Maltings, Mills, Manufactures, and all buildings calculated for Mercantile purposes ... every Lot will have immediate access to the railway by means of a tramway, and of the intended road upon which it will abut.

Every lot was sold and Sudbury's first industrial estate was established overnight. In 1865 the line was extended to Cambridge which meant crossing the Common Land and the money they paid the freemen was invested in purchasing part of North Meadow and Great Fulling Pit Meadow. The new station was situated closer to Friar's Meadow and an avenue approach made to link with the newly named Station Road. Between the old and new stations was a large goods and shunting yard with train sheds and an engine turntable. Tram-lines crossed Great Eastern Road from the goods yard to the warehouses opposite. Sidings ran parallel with Cornard Road to serve Oliver's brewery and Chilton brickworks with a spur line going under the road and into the pit. The station included the stationmaster's house, booking hall, waiting room, goods office and a WH Smiths bookstall.

Although it was a single line track there was space for a second track should it be necessary. This line was meant to connect the industrial Midlands with the East Anglian ports and during the war years it certainly served that purpose. It came as a great shock when the line from Sudbury to Cambridge closed in the 1960s on Dr Beeching's recommendation, particularly as both

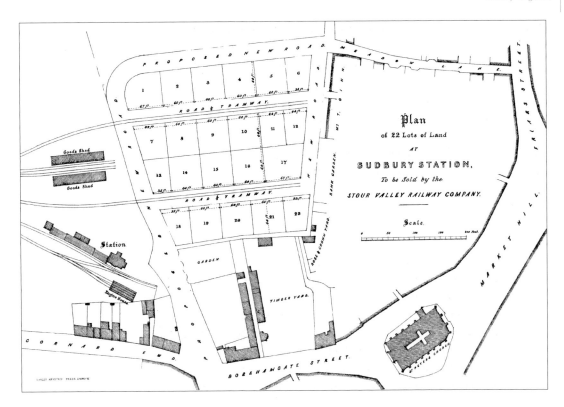

The railway arrived in 1849 and a huge area was laid out for warehouses with the advantage of rail track alongside. This was to be a bitter blow to the Stour Navigation as twenty-two plots of land was put up for auction at The Rose and Crown and every one was sold.

Haverhill and Sudbury were about to double their populations with an influx from London and were negotiating the introduction of new industries.

The Brickfields

Brick making in Sudbury, as we saw at St Gregory's church, has been more or less ongoing since Saxon times. For most of that time bricks were fired as and when required, in spite of what the textbooks may say, the skill was never lost. Bricks were being made at Ballingdon Grove in large numbers as early as the late eighteenth century and Elliston Allen, the proprietor, was the Stour Navigation's best customer. He had his own river cutting to the Grove works.

A brick kiln is mentioned in Ballingdon manor rolls of 1684 but the exact location is obscure. George Pung had started his brickworks in Sandy Lane in about 1805 and yet another and larger works, The Victoria Brickworks was established off the Bulmer Road in around 1830. Not surprisingly the great majority of labourers in Ballingdon were involved in the industry. Other brickworks were set up in other parts of Sudbury especially in the Chilton area. The Alexandra Works off Newton Road, at one time linked with the Victoria Works in Ballingdon, and the Chilton brickworks at Armes factory site in Cornard Road and the California brickworks in Waldingfield Road were all flourishing in the second half of the nineteenth century. Allens were producing bricks in a pit carved out of the Belle Vue estate in Cornard Road, very close to the station with a railway that passed under the road.

The railway was in direct competition with the Navigation in bringing coal into Sudbury to fire the kilns. At the Cornard Road works they could deliver the coal on site and the bricks could be loaded directly onto the trucks for delivery anywhere in the country. Nevertheless many of the bricks produced were needed locally as the towns streets reached out into the open countryside towards Melford and Waldingfield. The railway had stimulated other industries, especially malting and bricks were needed for the new maltings in Girling Street, Melford and the Station Maltings at Sudbury.

It all came to an end around the time of the First World War which contributed to a labour shortage as men left to fight for their country. But the end was in sight before then as building had slowed down and the demand eased off. The last brickworks to close was Grimwoods at Little Cornard which survived the Second World War by just a year or so.

Outside the town, at Bulmer, Peter Minter and his company are carrying on the tradition today by firing special bricks on demand. There are countless owners of historic brick buildings throughout the country who are regular customers and modern Bulmer bricks sit comfortably with Tudor originals and only Peter Minter can tell the difference!

Sudbury bricks were both red and white and the latter weathered to an attractive silver grey which is the one people tend to associate more with Ballingdon. There is a tendency for some people to attempt to clean their brickwork back to the original creamy white but this is a mistake, the weathered white brick is as traditional in Sudbury as the silvery oak is from the fifteenth-century timber-framed buildings.

The Ballingdon Millwrights

In the nineteenth century, at the foot of Ballingdon Hill, there was an enclave of millwrights, of which Ling Robinson was the oldest established. He was born in West House in 1759 and was operating as a millwright at that address in 1785. He married Sarah Johnson at All Saints on 7 December 1790 and they had five daughters and two sons. Ling died in 1816 aged fifty-seven. His two sons, George and Ling jnr, carried on the business together until George left to join William Farrow to work as journeyman millwrights.

Ling Robinson jnr continued the family business until 1846 or later. The yard from where they operated is called Robinson's Yard. Both father and son are buried in the nave at All Saints, at that time an honour reserved for well-respected persons.

Thomas Bear, millwright, arrived in Ballingdon in 1839 and five years later his son William took over the business and made it the largest firm of millwrights, squeezing out all other opposition. He moved to Sepulchre Street in 1855 and opened a branch at Ipswich ten years later. Eventually his Sudbury business moved to Station Road. He was a major importer of millstones from France.

William Bear's tower windmills were at Lavenham, Buxhall, Preston St Mary and Stansfield. He was also the builder of Highfield Smock Mill at Holgate in

Ballingdon Mill was a smock mill and sometimes called Kitchen Mill because it was on land belonging to Kitchen Farm. The Clover family worked it until it was struck by lightning and finally dismantled in the 1930s. The brick base has survived.

Sudbury. It stood 70ft high which enabled it to have large sails 55ft in length with three rows of shutters on each. The diameter of the sail sweep was therefore one 110ft which generated the power to drive four pairs of millstones. It was a most impressive sight with a three-storeyed brick base some 30ft in height with a 40ft timber structure on top of that. It was dismantled and the brick base converted into a house in 1927 which still stands.

There are eight millwrights listed in Ballingdon in the 1851 census. William Bear's premises in Ballingdon were just round the corner in Middleton Road backing on to the old brewery site. His Station Road premises became Barton's Engineers and subsequently Brunton's Propellers are now mostly demolished.

There were at least five windmills in Sudbury, two at the top of North Street of which one was on a site close to the Masonic Hall, after it was demolished the site was known as The Mount and cottages were built on it, they were demolished and replaced with an office block. The other mill stood opposite, where the lock-up shops are now, and gave its name to the Millfield which stretched from North Street car park to Gainsborough Road.

Ballingdon smock mill stood in Bulmer Road and was sometimes called Kitchen Mill which seems to suggest that it belonged to Kitchen Farm further up the road. The last owners were the Clover family who still lived in the mill house when my family moved to Ballingdon in 1941. The mill was struck by lightening and finally dismantled in the 1930s leaving the brick base and the mill house. The fourth mill was Highfield which we have already mentioned, and the fifth is shown on Brewer's map of 1714 off the Newton Road but nothing is known about it.

EAST VIEW OF OLD MOOT HALL, SUDBURY, SUFFOLK.
(From an Old Water Colour Drawing in the possession of Mr. G. Lancelot Andrewes.)

Very few pictures of the Moot Hall which stood on the Market Hill have survived. This was probably painted shortly before demolition. On the far left is The Swan where Dickens stayed and next door is the Coffee House Inn where the Corn Exchange was built.

Another industry established in the nineteenth century was the manufacture of coconut matting and the largest factory was Armes's in Cornard Road which had origianlly been built with bricks, made on the site, as a flour mill. William Armes set it up as a mat factory in 1884 and the family ran it until 1969 when the business was sold. The factory no longer makes coconut matting.

chapter eight

Twentieth century

When Victoria died in 1901 and her son became Edward VII, it was a complete novelty for the great majority of Sudburians to find themselves subjects of a male monarch. She had reigned for sixty-three years and there were not many who could remember the days of the old King, William IV, and even fewer recalled the days of his predecessor George IV, but there were a few. It is quite possible that one of them held in their hands a baby who would watch a man walk on the moon, such would be the speed of change.

There was not much change for the first ten years. Sudbury with a population of a little over 6,000 had become a busy market town with several thriving industries looking confidently into the future. The coronation of the king was celebrated with a huge outdoor party for children on the decorated Market Hill. A new police station was built at Borehamgate End in 1901, a fine building in terracotta and glazed brick which also contained living quarters for police officers. The following year saw another church built, this time for the Methodists at the foot of York Road, in the Gothic style, with flint walls and red brick trimmings, it suited the site perfectly.

The medieval Black Boy Inn on the Market Hill had acquired a Georgian façade in the late eighteenth century, the Edwardians replaced it with a mock-Tudor gable and bay windows in 1901. The George Inn in Old Market Place was demolished in 1908 and replaced with a startling red brick building for Walker's Stores, one of a national chain that would soon be followed by others, to the consternation of local shopkeepers.

The Market Hill was the setting for a funeral parade commemorating the death of the king in 1910 and for the subsequent coronation celebrations a year later. Then it became the focal point for another royal occasion on 10 June 1913 when HRH Princess Louise, Duchess of Argyll, the daughter of Queen Victoria, unveiled the Gainsborough statue as the national memorial to the great painter and presented it to the town of Sudbury.

The sculptor was Bertram Mackennal who had recently designed the coinage for George V. He was an Australian, born in Melbourne in 1863 and trained initially in Paris. He came to London in 1882 and had numerous commissions including recumbent effigies of Edward VII and Alexandra at Windsor. The bronze statue of Gainsborough is 8ft 6in high and mounted on a base of Portland stone. He is portrayed as he might have looked when painting, with palette and brush in hand and gazing towards his house in Gainsborough Street. The bronze panel on the front of the base is said to represent a woman of his time with a musical instrument in her hand but it is plainly a lady of the sculptor's time and the manner in which her dress falls out of the 'frame' makes this a work in the Art Nouveau style The statue is generally regarded as one of his finest works and it is signed with his initials on the tree trunk behind the seated lady. At the back of the stone base another bronze, in the form of a trophy of musical instruments, indicates the painter's love of music.

On the afternoon of 10 June 1913, HRH Princess Louise, Duchess of Argyll unveiled the national monument to Gainsborough. It was the sort of occasion the hill was meant for and it was packed to capacity.

The First World War

Every town and village in England was affected by this awful and bloody war as boatload after boatload of men were sent across the English Channel to fight. Patriotic fervour very soon turned to bitterness as the shocking toll of human life mounted and news of the conditions in which the men were fighting seeped through. This country was not invaded but it was shelled and bombarded from the sea on occasions, Lowestoft and Yarmouth in particular were to suffer. A new danger came in the form of airships or Zeppelins as they were more often called. These were intended to bomb the munitions factories in East Anglia but they did very little damage.

One of the biggest raids was in September 1916 when fourteen Zeppelins dropped approximately sixteen tons of bombs over East Anglia. Earlier, at the end of March, one of the airships strayed over Sudbury, even though there were no munitions factories in the area, and dropped a string of bombs. Some of them hit the terrace of Weavers Houses in East Street killing five people. Some of the houses were reduced from three to two storeys in height and are still to be seen today. The names of those who were killed were placed on the war memorial with those who died fighting abroad. In October 1921 the memorial was placed at the top of North Street but was subsequently moved to its present position by St Gregory's church.

The Rose and Crown Fire

The covered courtyard of The Rose and Crown Inn on the south side of St Peter's. It was the foremost inn in Sudbury with a rich historic past. Sadly it went up in flames in the early morning of New Year's Day 1922.

The Rose and Crown was Sudbury's foremost coaching inn that began life back in the days of the pilgrimages. It was first known as The Crown and became the Rose and Crown in Elizabeth's reign. Much of the original structure was concealed behind later Georgian work and it was built with a broad street frontage and long projecting wings at the rear. The wings formed a galleried court-yard which the Victorians sensibly gave a glass roof creating a winter-garden effect, enhanced with window boxes, climbing floral plants and singing caged birds. Not surprisingly it became the venue for most of the town's grand functions.

The inn presented a typical Georgian front to the street but the main structure was a fifteenth-century timber frame. Mr Winch saw his shop go up in flames but lost no time in securing vacant premises on the other side of the inn while the fire was still burning. His new shop is still there today.

In 1753 the Sudbury stagecoach was advertised as departing from The Rose and Crown every Monday, Wednesday and Friday for the Spread Eagle in Gracechurch Street, London. It called at The Bell in Castle Hedingham, The Green Man at Gosfield and The White Hart in Bocking and arrived at London the same day. The charge was nine shillings for each passenger that could include 30lbs of luggage.

In the 1840s there were five coaches leaving from its yard daily, two for Bury, two for London and one for Norwich. We must remember that Mr Pickwick himself 'took the coach to Bury' after the election at Eatanswill when The Rose and Crown became The Town Arms.

Disaster struck in the early morning of New Year's Day 1922 when the inn went up in flames. There was a strong westerly wind that day that caused the fire to spread towards King Street and thereby engulfing Winch's drapery shop next door and another drapery emporium called Manchester House. Not much further down King Street was Dixon Scott's hardware shop containing oils and gunpowder, then Wheeler's timber yard. Fire crews from as far away as Colchester attended but there was a shortage of water and much time was lost in fixing a long hose to bring water from the river. By then the hotel was totally destroyed and the firefighters concentrated on containing the blaze and prevent it from spreading further.

Volunteers took up positions on the roofs of St Peter's immediately opposite to ensure the safety of the building from sparks and burning debris. The astute Mr Winch, seeing his shop burned to the ground, was on the doorstep of the estate agent when it opened for business, and while the fire was still burning, to negotiate the purchase of vacant premises on the Market Hill just yards from his old shop. He was open for business within days and the firm still trades there.

It was the largest fire recorded in the town's history and it could have been even worse because soon after the blaze was put out the wind changed and blew from the east. Had that happened sooner then much of the Market Hill would also have been destroyed. For over ten years the site of the Rose and Crown remained vacant before the County Cinema was built on it.

Sudbury already had one cinema, The Gainsborough Theatre, built on the site of an old Maltings in 1912. Before that films were shown in a timber warehouse opposite which had its own DC generator. For the first few years the generator supplied electricity for the new cinema and the wires were suspended across the road. An illustration of the interior of the cinema in a trades exhibition programme of 1926 shows the walls of the auditorium decorated with landscape murals. It also had a sliding section in the roof which could be opened to ventilate the place, a common feature in music halls but very rarely seen in a cinema. The building is now used as a night-club and although the exterior has survived more or less intact the interior has been subjected to considerable alterations even though it is a listed building.

General Charles Gates Dawes, US Ambassador

The Market Hill once again served as a civic square on 1 October 1929 when the US Ambassador, General Dawes, was given the Honorary Freedom of the Borough of Sudbury in recognition of his ancestral connections with the town. Apparently it was discovered that the general was a direct descendant of William Dawes of the parish of All Saints who sailed to America in 1635 to begin a new life here. It is quite plain from the correspondence between the mayor and the ambassador that the latter was expecting a quiet little ceremony.

He underestimated the strength of civic pride in the small country town. Gradually he began to realise just what he had agreed to accept and there was no going back. The mayor, Edward Page Fitzgerald, represented a town with over 2,000 years of history and one which had played a part in the founding of America. There were no trade deals involved, there was no hidden agenda, they simply wanted to give recognition to the fact that a man whose roots were in Sudbury was now the United States Ambassador to London. He went along with it and Sudbury did him proud.

Apart from the Freedom of the Borough he was presented with a model of a New England room with the appropriate furniture made by the carpenters at P.S. Head on the Market Hill. Mrs Dawes was presented with an embroidered cushion made from Sudbury silk. There was a long procession down the Market Hill to the Drill Hall in Gainsborough Street where lunch was served and then he visited Gainsborough's house before departing. Most of the national press were present and all the events were covered in the newspapers the next morning. The following week the Gainsborough Cinema was packed as everything was shown again on the silver screen.

Adrian Bell's Sudbury

Earlier in that same year a rather formidable, middle-aged lady by the name of Mrs Bell was house-hunting in Sudbury. She wanted a house in the area within walking distance of the station from where her husband, a journalist, could commute to London. She came across No. 1 Stour Street, then called The Gables, peered through the windows and liked what she saw. She decided at once to rent it and within days she and her husband had moved in.

They were a middle-class couple from London whose son Adrian had visited Suffolk and fallen in love with it. Not only that but, apparently to her horror, he had expressed a wish to be a farmer. He subsequently served an apprenticeship on a farm at Stradishall after which his parents assisted him in buying a small farm of his own. They had even moved up to Suffolk to be near him but shortly before the house-hunting trip to Sudbury, their son, Adrian, had given up the farm. Now that his parents had found a new home he reluctantly moved in with them.

For Adrian it was a time to take stock and to decide where his future lay. He still wanted to farm but there had been some pressure to take up journalism and he did have a gift for writing. He decided to put down in writing his experiences as a farmer and although there was no shortage of rooms at The Gables he set up the garden house as his study and commenced to write. In 1931 his first book *Corduroy* was published to be followed by two others, *Silver Ley* and *The Cherry Tree*, all to much acclaim. He later described his period in Sudbury with much affection in his biography *My Own Master*, published in 1961.

Adrian was also skilled at compiling crosswords and through journalist friends of his father it was suggested that he might compile one for *The Times*. He did so and as a result the garden house has another claim to fame. The very first *Times* crossword was compiled within its walls.

The Second World War and Sudbury

In November 1941 the 1st Battalion London Scottish Regiment were stationed at Sudbury. They were billeted all over the town, some were at The Red House, and some occupied the Old Moot Hall in Cross Street, while others moved into a disused silk factory immediately opposite the Drill Hall which served as their HQ. They had a superb pipe band which came into its own at the church parade on the Market Hill on Sunday mornings. Shortly after the parade the pipe band would return to the hill and stand in a circle and play. They stayed in Sudbury until the following June.

486th Bombardment Group (H)

In 1943 some intense activity began at the top of Gallows Hill and around Chilton. It began with the cutting down of trees along the roadside by the local timber merchants and the removal of hedges. They were building an airfield.

Lorry loads of gravel thundered past the doors in Ballingdon dripping water over a road already spattered with chalk from Sandy Lane pit and cow dung from Braybrooks cows which were brought off the meadows for milking.

After the building of the runways up went the Nissen huts and the big hangers and the airfield was finished in remarkably quick time. On Wednesday 5 April, from four in the morning until nine in the evening, men of the 486th Bombardment Group arrived at 'AAF Station 174 Sudbury'. The Americans had arrived. During the next few days their aircraft flew in and training for combat commenced. By May the base was fully operational and bombing missions began.

They flew a total of 191 missions between May 1944 and April 1945 in Liberators and Fortresses. There were some 2,800 servicemen on the base and 400 of them were killed in action and this was only one of almost a hundred such bases across East Anglia.

They had their own American Red Cross Service Club in the town centre at East House, the old home of Mrs Sykes, granddaughter of Robert Andrews of the Gainsborough portrait fame. On Tuesday 8 May 1945 the war was over in Europe. There were victory celebrations, dancing on the Market Hill, street parties and bonfires. During the next two months there was a general winding down at the airbase, the planes flew out and did not return and the expansive skies of East Anglia, which painters love so much, became quiet again. Some of the Americans had married local girls who were soon referred to as GI brides, but it would be a while before they settled down because the Pacific War was not yet over. And the war was not over for the many families whose relatives were serving in Burma and India, especially the 4th and 5th Battalions of the Suffolk Regiment who were at Singapore when it fell to the Japanese. VJ Day came on the 15 August and it was the autumn before the survivors returned. The names of those who did not return were inscribed on the war memorial. Another memorial to the Americans who served in the 486th Bombardment Group (H) and the 400 who gave their lives in the cause of freedom, was dedicated in 1987.

Conclusions

In the half century since the war the town has seen many changes and they can only be mentioned here briefly for want of space.

1960s Town Clearances

All the weaving terraces in Gregory Street, The Croft, and Church Walk were demolished for road widening and Gooseberry Row went for car parking. East House was replaced by a new post office. The Edwardian police station was cleared for a traffic roundabout and Mill Lane was completely removed for school extensions. A new one-way traffic system was adopted and a new road driven through from Girling Street to Newton Road. Sudbury and Great Cornard with Haverhill received 'London Overspill' and new housing estates were built to accommodate them and Borehamgate precinct was built.

1970s to the Present

In 1974 Sudbury lost its status as a borough and came under the newly formed Babergh District Council. It was hoped that Sudbury would become the administration centre but that honour went to Hadleigh because it was in a geographically more central position. The lovely Georgian warehouses at the quay have been converted, one is the Quay Theatre, the other is the headquarters of the River Stour Trust. The Quay Basin has been restored and the whole area with its access to the valley walk and Friar's Meadows is a precious asset.

New town houses have appeared in the Saxon lanes that are still quiet but there is too much traffic in the other historic streets and twenty-five years of waiting for a by-pass were still unresolved in 2004. Until that problem is solved Sudbury will not be able to fully exploit its tourist potential but nonetheless it does attract visitors from all over the world because, in spite of everything, the old town below the Market Hill has survived relatively intact, all the modern development is to the north and east and expanding fast.

Too often in the past Sudbury was overshadowed by Long Melford and Lavenham but that is no longer the case. It is fast being appreciated for its own worth and much of the credit for that is due to an exceptional Tourist Information Centre at the town hall.

Walking tour

Market Hill, Old Market Place, King Street (Borehamgate)

These three areas were planned as open spaces, with the siting of St Peter's church at the centre as a focal point and a symbol of a prosperous market town. It was a deliberate and successful piece of fourteenth-century town planning and must be viewed as such to fully appreciate what we have. The Victorians understood it when they removed all the buildings that encroached on the site and for a few years Sudbury regained its civic square. Now it has been completely sacrificed to the needs of modern traffic and has been reduced to a car park.

Old Market Place

This is the area in front of the town hall which replaced the Saxon market place in Stour Street. The Butter Cross stood at the centre and a few yards to the east was The Cage in which people causing a disturbance were placed. The space would be filled with stalls on market days. The stallholders would pay their dues at the Exchequer Office, which in turn became the Chequers Inn until the town hall was built on the site by Thomas Ginn in 1826-28. Against the church railings is a horse trough and dog trough which has gained international recognition since Dodie Smith had Pongo and Missis drinking from it in *One Hundred and One Dalmatians*.

King Street (Borehamgate)

This wide street is east of the church and was the meat market. By the fifteenth-century butcher's shambles, or permanent stalls, stood in the centre. Borehamgate is a corruption of Bar and Gate marking the end of the town at this

117

opposite Stour Street: medieval cottages at the very centre of the Saxon town (above), and facing the site of the old Saxon Market (below).

right St Peter's tower dominates the town centre. It was given a copper spire in 1810 but it was removed in the 1960s when the belfry stage had to be rebuilt.

point. No. 2 King Street, the large mansion house with the Doric porch was built by a Sudbury mayor, Thomas Jones in 1816 on the site of a house called The Balcony and The Cock Inn. Across the road from him was The Rose and Crown (see p.112) burned down in 1922 and was replaced by the County Cinema and a parade of shops. The cinema was demolished in the 1960s but the shops remain. Borehamgate precinct was built in the 1960s on the site of Borehamgate House and a timber yard. Beyond the trees in the background and off Newton Road is Belle Vue park, a pleasant oasis in the heart of town. The original house built in the eighteenth century by Nathaniel Burrough, a retired City of London grocer and cousin of Thomas Gainsborough. He modelled it on a house he admired in Green Park, London. It was demolished in the nineteenth century by a Mr Canham and the present, less attractive, house built on its site. The church looks most impressive when approaching the town from this end.

Market Hill

Market Hill is to the west of the church and is the setting for the market on Thursdays and Saturdays. It is no accident that the west doors beneath the soaring tower of St Peters open out on to this superb open space that linked the old town to the new. In all probability it was intended for the site of the two annual fairs which later transferred to The Croft, just as Angel Hill at Bury was the site of the famous Bury Fair. It was encroached on in the sixteenth century when the Moot Hall was built at the lower end in the reign of Mary.

Gainsborough's statue (see p.110), and the library (see p.98) are here in the company of several fine buildings. On the south side No. 30, Lloyds Bank, is the first house to be built entirely of brick in Sudbury, built by the Revd Henry

Crossman for his daughter on her marriage to Edward Green of Lawford Hall in 1768. No. 28, two doors up, is an original narrow fourteenth-century building with an early nineteenth-century frontage with a Regency Gothic window on the first floor and a handsome cast iron balcony screen. Further up Nos 23-4, presently an estate agent's office, has an excellent fifteenth-century interior with carved doorways and moulded beams but a Victorian façade. Next door at No. 22 are the premises Winches moved into when their shop in King Street was burned with the Rose and Crown in 1922 (see p.112). This is a pleasant nine-teenth century frontage but there is much exposed medieval timber inside, some of it fourteenth century. A surviving eighteenth-century shop front has been moved to the side in recent years.

On the other side of Lloyds Bank, on the site of the Swan Inn with its Pickwick associations, (see p.98) is Westminster Bank in the Georgian style of 1903 by Cheston and Perkins and just beyond the library is Barclays Bank. This is a splendid high quality brick building in the Queen Anne style by B. Binyon in 1879. These are two splendid examples, and an object lesson to modern architects, on how to approach infilling in a medieval country town.

On the north side of the hill are considerable remains of medieval timber framing concealed behind later façades. At the foot of the hill at Nos 1-3 is a substantial fifteenth-century house, at one time the home of the Hassel family who had sugar plantations in the West Indies and were leading citizens in the eighteenth century. Several of them are buried in All Saints church. Just inside the door of No. 4 can be seen the oldest shop window in Sudbury with sixteenth-century timber which tells us an alley ran alongside this building at one time. It is otherwise a very nice restrained Regency façade with four round-headed windows on the first floor. Behind the mock-Tudor façade of the Black Boy is the genuine article although a splendid Jacobean fireplace and over-mantle was removed from here to Salter's Hall in 1901. The remaining build-ings mostly have neat plain, early nineteenth-century façades to comply with the Town Improvement Act of 1826 (see p.95).

Every now and then some well meaning person comes up with a plan for Market Hill, such as planting trees or paving areas with water features and the like. All it needs is to have the through traffic removed so that it can become the civic and public open space it was designed to be from the start.

Walking the Ditch – Friar's Street to the Croft

This walk follows the line of the Saxon ditch and takes about forty-five minutes. Enter Friar's Street at the foot of Market Hill and you are now in the ditch, it was 21 metres wide and 3 metres deep with a rampart 6 metres high on your right. Friar's Street commences at Station Road and is one of the most attractive streets in the town. At the commencement of it is The Anchor Inn, Sudbury's oldest inn and a most interesting building of two distinctive styles and dates.

The earliest reference to The Anchor as an inn is in 1651 when Thomas Polley provided a charity whereby ten dozen loaves were distributed to the poor from the proceeds 'of a house called The Anchor'. In 1724 Susan Girling left the property on trust to supply fifty shirts and fifty smocks yearly for those receiving coats through Carter's Charity. Before then it was a fourteenth-century cloth merchant's house. In 1776 a section of the neighbouring White Hart Inn containing its first floor assembly room was annexed and thus doubled the width of the frontage. The rest of the White Hart was demolished. In the yard, plays were performed and after the Restoration a barn was provided for strolling players to perform in. It is now converted into a cottage.

Upstairs at No. 5 is a recently uncovered mural probably painted at the end of the seventeenth century by an itinerant artist. Following the curve of the ditch is a nice run of eighteenth-century stuccoed houses, especially fine is No. 31 and next door to it is the little cottage where Thomas Gainsborough the artist lived on his return to Sudbury and where his daughters were born (see p.82). Go down Bullocks Lane to see The Red House with its serpentine garden wall and gazebo. With luck you will see the garden gate of 'The Friars' open and observe a Gothic window forming a garden feature and brought here from the Priory House when it was demolished.

The curve continues to Priory Gate (see p.21) and comes to an end at Church Street but the ditch continued through the school and we follow it by using the footpath skirting the playground. It brings us to Mill Hill where the ditch entered the river into the mill pool. Pass in front of the Mill Hotel on to the Common and follow the Mill Leat which was part of the ditch formed by the diverted river. Pass through the floodgates and to Croft Bridge which should be crossed to The Croft and follow the path in a straight line to Croft Road by the traffic lights and into Burkitts Lane which will bring you back to where we started. You will have now completely encircled the Saxon town.

Inside the Rampart – a quiet walk in Saxon streets

This walk follows the rampart inside the town and helps to appreciate the original plan. Enter the old town from Market Hill into Gainsborough (Sepulchre) Street. After just a few yards enter Christopher Lane on the left. Immediately on your left is the site of The Angel Inn which gave this lane its eighteenth-century name of Angel Back Lane. Before that it was Wylewerlelane. On the right is The Christopher once owned by Thomas Gainsborough's maternal grandparents and now The Christopher Resources Centre. The lane is almost traffic free and runs parallel with the ditch and rampart which would have been on the left. On the right is William Wood House now sheltered accommodation but once the grammar school (see p.67). At the end of the lane we cross School Street into Straw Lane (Stewards Lane)which will bring us to Plough Lane. By now you will have noticed that these lanes have no pavements. Enter the footpath alongside the school playground to Mill Hill and cross the road with care to Walnuttree Lane and continue until you come to St Gregory's church. Cross the busy one-way street and turn left into Church Walk by The Waggon and Horses. This leads into Acton Green and Weavers Lane to the point where we started.

St Gregory's flint and stone chequer work in the north aisle of about 1360 which was restored later by Butterfield.

St Gregory's angel from the chancel ceiling holding the crown of thorns.

Across Town – Gainsborough Street, Stour Street, Cross Street, Church Street.

You will share this walk with the traffic so evenings and Sundays are the best. Enter Gainsborough Street at the foot of Market Hill and notice immediately Burkitt's House on the corner of Burkitt's Lane. An eighteenth-century house with a nineteenth-century top floor added. Notice the fanlight over the door that forms Edward Burkitt's initials. Much of the older house is incorporated within. The Burkitts were cloth merchants and deeply religious. John Bunyan is said to have preached in their kitchen here. Next door, No. 53 is part of the original Burkitt House and has much exposed timber inside.

Further down on the corner of Weavers Lane is a three-storeyed silk weaving factory now converted to office use. It was operating at the end of the eighteenth century when it was annexed to No. 46, Gainsborough's house (see p.85). The pavements narrow as we approach and reach the crossroads. This is the centre of the Saxon town. Gregory Street to the right leads to the church and the Croft. School Street, on the left, goes down to Friar's Street. On the corner of Gregory Street is the site of St Sepulchre's chapel (see p.16).

Opposite is Stour Street and on the corner is the house called 'The Stone'. In the fifteenth century it was called Stone Hall and was the home of Thomas Shorthose (see p.59) who gave money to All Saints church. Later it was the house of Thomas Carter, the clothier who is buried in St Gregory's church (see p.49) and was 'The Sudbury Camel that passed through the eye of a needle'. In the 1920s it was rented by Mr and Mrs Bell (see p.114) and their son Adrian, acclaimed for a trilogy of books about his farming experiences in Suffolk. Facing this house was the Saxon market place.

There are several good timber-framed houses but the finest are the range known as Salter's Hall and Chantry, best seen from the opposite side of the road. They were mostly built around 1450 but the third gable is clearly earlier. These are houses of extremely high quality of which Salter's Hall is the finest. All the windows have retained their original carved wooden tracery. Especially fine is the oriel window beneath the gable with its carved soffit showing St James the

All Saints tower with massive stair turret is regarded by many as the finest of Sudbury's three medieval church towers.

Detail of the soffit, an elephant, at St James the Less, with his fulling club, and a lion.

Detail of the jettied first floor at Cleeve Hall, The gables were removed in the eighteenth century.

Less between an elephant and a lion. The builder of this house may well have been the owner of a fulling mill. The hill was made less steep in the 1820s by McAdam.

Opposite Salter's Hall is Cleeve Hall, originally Stour Hall (hence medieval Stourhall Street) then renamed Springfield Lodge. This is almost certainly the site of the original Sudbury Manor. At one time this house had gables but they were removed and the hipped roofs were added in the middle of the eighteenth century.

At the foot of the hill on the right is the former home of the Sparrow family which has recently been restored. It became a tannery but it is interesting because it was built on the edge of the ditch which joined the river here. Further into Cross Street and half way down on the right Nos 75-8 represents a seventeenth-century weaving complex purchased by Abraham Griggs on his marriage to Susannah, Thomas Gainsborough's aunt, in 1698. He employed outworkers

Gainsborough's House, the birthplace of the painter Thomas Gainsborough in 1727. This Georgian façade was built for his father two years previously to conceal the unfashionable medieval timber-framed building behind.

in the cloth industry and this complex became The Warehouse. The family were to flourish until the nineteenth century. (see p.85) producing bunting for the Royal Navy.

The Stars and Stripes which flew over Fort Lauderdale and inspired the words of the American national anthem was made with bunting supplied by this warehouse and woven by Sudbury girls. No. 78 was the family house of Abraham Griggs in the seventeenth century.

Further down across the road is The Old Moot Hall, used as such before the later hall was built on Market Hill in the reign of Mary Tudor. There is some evidence that this building continued to be used for civic purposes in the reign of James I. His arms are painted on the chimney breast of a downstairs chamber. It has been suggested that this was the home of Mayor Wells in the fifteenth century but there is no evidence to support this. It is an exceptional building and well maintained by the present owners.

Across the road again is Noah's Ark Lane, so called, perhaps, because the cattle went down it to the common two by two. It is worth going on to Portmanscroft to view the back of Cross Street towards All Saints tower, it is a view that has not changed in 400 years. At the end of Cross Street is Ballingdon Bridge and the river, however, we turn now into Church Street, pass the Ballingdon Bull, built in around 1540 and through All Saints churchyard (see p.62) and so link up with Friar's Street which will take us back to the town centre.

The Croft to Brundon and back via the Valley Walk

This is a lovely walk – wear some sensible shoes. Start from Croft Bridge and turn right to follow the river footpath to Brundon Hall partly hidden behind trees. This is a medieval hall encased and enlarged in Georgian red brick in around 1730 by the Windhams of Felbrigg who owned it.

The path passes round the hall and leads to the mill and mill cottages. These were all built for the Windhams by Kingsbury of Boxford, a firm which existed until 1984. This is a most picturesque sight, 'more Constable than Constable' and, perhaps, fortunately not painted by him or the peace of this delightful corner would be more often disturbed than it is.

Either cross the bridge and return via North Meadows and Melford Road or follow the lane round until you reach a bridge over the old rail track which is now the Valley Walk. Move down to the track and follow it back to Sudbury, there are various points where one can get off, The Common at Ballingdon, The Quay Basin, or Friar's Meadow near the station.

Bibliography

Bell, Adrian, *My Own Master* (Faber and Faber, 1961)

Belsey, Hugh, *Gainsborough's Family* (Exhibition catalogue, Gainsborough's House Society, 1988)

Berry, Alan, *Eighteenth Century Sudbury* (Suffolk County Council, Arts and Libraries, 1992)

Cooper, Ashley, *Heart of our History Vol. 1* (Bulmer Historical Society, 1994)

Cooper, Ashley, *Our Mother Earth Vol. 2* (Bulmer Historical Society, 1998)

Cross, Peter, *The Lady in Medieval England* (Sutton Publishing, 1998)

Felton, Mrs Phylis, *Walnuttree Hospital and The Sudbury Workhouse* (unpublished notes)

Fletcher, Richard, *Who's Who in Roman Britain and Anglo Saxon England* (Shepheard-Walwyn, 1989)

Hayes, John, *Thomas Gainsborough* (Exhibition catalogue, Tate Gallery Publications Dept., 1980)

Mortimer, Richard, *Charters of St Bartholomew's Sudbury* (Suffolk Records Society, Boydell Press, 1996)

Perry, Walter, *The Millwrights of Ballingdon* (unpublished research, Sudbury History Society)

Sperling, F.C.D., *Hodson's History of the Borough of Sudbury* (1896)

Stokes, Ethel and Redstone, Lilian, *Calender of the Muniments of the Borough of Sudbury* (Suffolk Institute of Archeology & Natural History, 1909)

Tyerman, Christopher, *Who's Who in Early Medieval England* (Shepheard-Walwyn, 1996)

Victoria County History, Suffolk

Waller, Ambrose J.R., *The Suffolk Stour* (Norman Adlard & Co. Ltd (Ipswich), 1957)

Wardman, John, *Sudbury Common Lands* (Sudbury Common Lands Charity, 1996)

Woods, William, *England in the Age of Chaucer* (Hart-Davis, MacGibbon, 1976)

Index